How to Use This Book

Congratulations! You are stepping out onto a life-changing journey. As you begin to tend the fire of your soul, your passion for experiencing God will grow; and your faith will become the most meaningful part of your life. *Soul Tending: Life-Forming Practices for Older Youth and Young Adults* can be used in many ways and in several different settings to set the maximum number of people "on fire" for God!

Who Should Use *Soul Tending*?

Soul Tending is for young people in senior high school or college, although other adults may want to tend the fires of their souls, as well.

How to Use *Soul Tending*

The ideal setting for using *Soul Tending* is within a small group. If you are currently in a small group, then you are ready to begin! If not, gather some fellow seekers and find a regular meeting time.

You'll want to use *Soul Tending* along with your Bible and a pen. We've left enough space in the book for you to write down your answers to certain questions. Some activities, though, suggest more thoughtful journaling exercises. It's probably a good idea to purchase a separate journal or notebook where you can record those insights, expanding on the impressions of your journey.

What Does a Small Group Meeting Look Like?

Your meetings will last as long as you decide because you will design them. The simple and easy-to-remember SPIRIT format adapts to the needs and passions of your group:

 **igns of the Spirit**

You'll begin each meeting by spending a few minutes discussing God's activity in your life through the previous week with the questions:

- ❖ Where have you seen God's Spirit at work this week?
- ❖ How have you experienced God's grace in a new way through Christian practice over the last week?
- ❖ How is it with your soul?

You'll also evaluate the previous week's practices and any joys or struggles that came about.

 **urpose**

Then, your small group will recite together a statement of purpose for the group.

 nstruction

You will spend the majority of your small group meeting time in this section, which will include an introduction to the practice you have chosen. Each week you will need to designate a facilitator to have read ahead to lead the session. You will find helpful directions that will alert you to group discussion questions, instructions to read aloud, and opportunities to talk with a partner.

 ehearsal

Each session offers you an opportunity to rehearse the practice in your small group. This way you will be able to work out any feelings of discomfort or clear up any confusion you may have about a practice. If the practice does not lend itself to a small group rehearsal, then you will find questions to help you talk through together how the practice will work.

 nvolving

This section will help you discuss the ways in which practicing your faith will affect all areas of your life—from your home life to your school life to your work life, and so forth.

 omorrow

In each session, you will be given several options of how you could engage the practice throughout your week. You will choose one option and commit to the practice. Consider this an act of accountability to the group.

Closing the Meeting

You will need to decide on a closing ritual that is unique to your group. Perhaps you will choose to share prayer requests, light a Christ candle, or sing "your" song. Let the closing ritual take on the identity of your group!

Getting Started

Before you begin exploring the individual practices of faith, read the introduction (on page 15) and use the discussion guide (on page 25) for your first meeting. After you have done that, you are ready to begin. Soul Tending is designed for each small group to chart its own course through the study. Start on any practice and stay on any practice as long as you like. You will find recommended resources in the Appendix on page 190, should you choose to go deeper into the Christian practices.

Soul Tending

Life-Forming Practices for Older Youth and Young Adults

Anne Broyles
Beverly Burton
Ken Carter
Rachel Cousart
Drew A. Dyson
Dennis J. Meaker
Barbara K. Mittman
Kara Lassen Oliver
Robin Pippin
Kyle Roberson
Soozung Sa
Amy Scott Vaughn
Jennifer A. Youngman

SOUL TENDING: LIFE-FORMING PRACTICES FOR OLDER YOUTH AND YOUNG ADULTS

All Scripture quotations, unless otherwise noted, are taken from the *New Revised Standard Version of the Bible*, copyright 1989, Division of Christian Education of the National Council of Churches of Christ in the United States of America. Used by permission. All rights reserved.

Scripture quotations marked (CEV) are from the Contemporary English Version Copyright © 1991, 1992, 1995 by American Bible Society. Used by permission.

Scripture quotations marked (Message) are taken from *THE MESSAGE*. Copyright © Eugene H. Peterson, 1993, 1994, 1995. Used by permission of NavPress Publishing Group.

Scripture quotations marked (NIV) are taken from HOLY BIBLE, NEW INTERNATIONAL VERSION®. NIV®. Copyright © 1973, 1978, 1984 by International Bible Society. Used by permission of Zondervan Publishing House. All rights reserved.

Scripture quotations marked (TANAKH) are from The TANAKH: The New JPS Translation According to the Traditional Hebrew Text. Copyright 1985 by the Jewish Publication Society. Used by permission.

02 03 04 05 06 07 08 09 10 11— 10 9 8 7 6 5 4 3 2 1

Contents

Life-Forming Practices

Life-forming practices are
our ordinary actions and human attempts
at being holy
through which God transforms us
into Christ's likeness
and grants us extraordinary grace
and bountiful blessings.

You may have heard the expressions "spiritual disciplines," "Christian practices," "means of grace," "practices of the faith," or even some other combination of those words. In this book we use them interchangeably to mean life-forming practices that God uses to make us more like Christ.

Jesus has said, "I came that … [you] may have life, and have it abundantly" (John 10:10). Life-forming practices help us to live that abundant life as we seek to be connected in every way and every action to God's love and grace.

On the soul tending journey, you will be enriched, renewed, and most importantly, formed in Christ.

Meet the Writers

Anne Broyles enjoyed many years of youth ministry. The highlight of her work with youth was five summers spent leading Sierra Service Project work teams to Native American reservations in the western United States. She is a retired United Methodist minister, best known for her writing in the field of spiritual formation. Her book, *Journaling: A Spiritual Journey* (Upper Room), has been a bestseller since 1988 and is printed in Korean. Anne lives in Malibu, California, and has two children, Trinity, age 20, and Justus, age 17.

Beverly Burton is a professional storyteller. She is a member of Mount Tabor United Methodist Church in Winston-Salem, North Carolina, where she serves as an adult leader with the youth ministry. She and her husband, Blaine, are parents of two teenage boys, Wesley and Andy.

Ken Carter is senior pastor of Mount Tabor United Methodist Church in Winston-Salem, North Carolina. He has written books on spiritual gifts and stewardship and writes regularly for *Reel to Real: Making the Most of the Movies With Youth* and *Reel Faith: Where Meaning Meets the Movies*, both published by Abingdon Press. He and his wife, Pam, are parents of two teenage girls, Elizabeth and Abby.

Rachel Cousart is a high school student preparing to enter college. She is an active participant in the youth leadership team, the youth choir, and the handbell choir of Mount Tabor United Methodist Church in Winston-Salem, North Carolina.

Drew A. Dyson is currently serving as the executive director of the Shared Mission Focus on Young People in Nashville, Tennessee. He is a commissioned elder in the greater New Jersey Annual Conference of The United Methodist Church. Dyson has a bachelors degree in youth ministry from Eastern College in St. Davids, Pennsylvania, and a master of divinity degree from Princeton Theological Seminary in Princeton, New Jersey. Previously, Drew has served as associate pastor and director of youth and young adult ministries at the Bridgewater United Methodist Church and director of youth ministries for the Ocean Grove Camp Meeting Association.

Dennis J. Meaker is a United Methodist pastor currently serving a small urban church in Nashville, Tennessee. He holds a master of divinity degree from Vanderbilt Divinity School and a juris doctor degree from the University of Tennessee. Dennis is a second career pastor, having practiced law in Tennessee for eighteen years.

Barbara K. Mittman is an ordained deacon, certified in Christian education and youth ministry. Barb currently serves as one of the pastors at First United Methodist Church in Ames, Iowa. She has also served on conference and local church program staffs. She has previously published church school curriculum for youth and authored two volumes of the *20/30 Bible Study for Young Adults*, published by Abingdon Press. Barb, her husband Bob, and daughter Katie live in Nevada, Iowa.

Kara Lassen Oliver serves as the project coordinator of the United Methodist Youth Organization. She advocates for youth, interpreting their concerns and convictions throughout The United Methodist Church. A graduate of Vanderbilt Divinity School, Kara lives and works in Nashville with her husband, Jeffrey, and daughter, Claire Marin.

Robin Pippin is founding editor of *Devo'Zine*, a devotional magazine published by The Upper Room. Her current title is editorial director of *Devo'Zine* and youth and young adult resources at The Upper Room. She writes about and leads workshops on writing, spiritual practices, and youth spirituality. She lives in Nashville, Tennessee, is married to Tim Pippin, and has three children, ages 13, 10, and 6.

Kyle Roberson currently serves as director of student ministries at University Park United Methodist Church in Dallas, Texas. Kyle and his wife, Joy, are also pursuing their master of divinity degrees at Perkins School of Theology in Dallas, Texas. Kyle graduated from Centenary College of Louisiana and is endorsed by the Centenary School of Church Careers. He has worked in youth ministry in Louisiana, Alabama, and Texas.

Soozung Sa is director of ministries with families and singles with the family and life span team at the General Board of Discipleship of The United Methodist Church in Nashville, Tennessee. She is completing a master of divinity degree at Vanderbilt Divinity School. As a child of a retired Korean United Methodist pastor reared in a bi-cultural Korean-American home, she also has great interest in the dynamics of being Asian American in the United States.

Amy Scott Vaughn is director of leadership development for the Princeton Theological Seminary Institute for Youth Ministry. An ordained Presbyterian Church (USA) minister, Vaughn formerly served as associate pastor for youth and Christian education at First Presbyterian Church in Cranbury, New Jersey. She coedited a series of curriculum resources to accompany the new catechisms of the Presbyterian Church (USA).

Jennifer A. Youngman is a development editor of youth resources for The United Methodist Publishing House. She holds a master of theological studies degree from Garrett-Evangelical Theological Seminary. Jenny lives in Nashville with her husband, Mark, and dogs, Wrigley Field, and Roxanne.

Acknowledgments

This book owes its life to *The Godbearing Life:*
The Art of Soul Tending for Youth Ministry,
by Kenda Creasy Dean and Ron Foster.
Their burning image has ignited a passion worth tending.

I would like to thank Mary Bernard, Crys Zinkiewicz,
Keely Moore, and Sheila Hewitt
for their faithful dedication to SOUL TENDING.

Thanks also to the SOUL TENDING development team
members—Glandion Carney, Drew Dyson, Barbara K.
Mittman, Kara Lassen Oliver, Joy Roberson, Kyle Roberson,
and Soozung Sa—for their longing to see
Christ formed in the lives of young persons.

—Jennifer A. Youngman, Editor

Foreword

Defining *spirituality* is a little like nailing paint to a wall. A definition always slides away from us somehow, too goopy or formless to lend itself to being captured by words. If American marketing is any indication, today the term *spiritual* can apply to everything from good business practice to color versions of personal video games. Nobody wants to be religious, but just about everybody wants to be "spiritual"—even though we're not always sure what that means.

In 1962, David and Sally Elkind asked young adolescents where they were most likely to experience God. Most of them said, "In a church or synagogue." By 1999, only one in seven adolescents told Gallup they thought being part of a religious community such as a mosque, synagogue, or church was necessary to being religious. Like "the Force" in the *Star Wars* movies, contemporary spirituality seems to consist of equal parts intuition, emotional stimulation, and a vague trust in a "higher power" that somehow add up to the Jedi belief that "the Force is with us." Few of us ask about the source of the Force.

Christians are different on two counts. First, Christian spirituality has a definite content. Christian spirituality means moving closer to Jesus Christ, not in the sense of "feeling" closer to him (that sometimes happens and sometimes doesn't in Christian practices), but in the sense of aligning our lives more closely to the image of God (*imago dei*) in Jesus Christ. Thomas á Kempis (1380–1471) called this "the imitation of Christ," but he didn't mean photocopying Jesus' every move. He meant identifying with Jesus, seeing and hearing the world through God's eyes and ears, entering the world as Jesus' body and blood, until Jesus' desires become our desires, his love becomes our love, and his life becomes our life. When we are baptized, his name even becomes our name—*Christ*ian—meaning that we start sharing a family resemblance with him. That's not because of our sin-dipped DNA, of course (after all, we're adopted), but because of the life-shaping actions we engage in together as the family of Jesus Christ.

> Only God's gift of grace makes the Christian life possible—grace poured out for us in small containers we call Christian practices, which are God's way of giving us living water in cups from which we can drink and in cups we can carry to others.

Obviously, we can't just "will" ourselves into imitating Christ, although most of us have tried. Jesus' self-giving love goes against every self-serving human instinct we have. As long as we view spirituality in terms of our effort instead of God's effort, we will fail. Only God's gift of grace makes the Christian life possible—grace poured out for us in small containers we call Christian practices. These are God's way of giving us living water in cups from which we can drink and in cups we can carry to others.

Offering living water to others leads to the second way Christian spirituality differs from "*Star Wars* spirituality." Although our relationship with Jesus Christ is intensely personal (after all, Jesus was a person), life with God is never an individual matter. Frederick Buechner says that minding one's own business is impossible for Christians. One way H. Richard Niebuhr describes the church in *The Meaning of Revelation* is a community from which Christian spirituality always grows. In the church we practice our faith alongside other people looking in the same direction, at the same reality of the cross. From the first century church of Acts until now, people who follow Jesus have come together in communities to practice their faith—to worship God with their lives as well as with their lips.

The daily, routine, seemingly "ordinary" practices of the Christian faith form a way of life for the believer and are at the heart of this book: They are the cups of grace from which we drink. Prayer. Hospitality. Keeping the Sabbath. Giving thanks. Almsgiving. Sacraments. Worship. Bible study. Spiritual friendship. Solitude. The editors of SOUL TENDING have created for you an outside-the-box book, a book meant to be "un-read" and translated into reflective actions to help you plumb the depths of God.

> The editors of SOUL TENDING have created for you an outside-the-box book, a book meant to be "un-read" and translated into reflective actions to help you plumb the depths of God.

These practices of Christian faith will set you apart (which is the definition of holiness). They will make you "odd" in our society, because imitating the self-giving love of Jesus Christ looks very different from the practices of self-fulfillment encouraged by consumer culture. You will have to be up for this. The pressures to cave in and the temptations to quit have, historically, been reasons why Christians have practiced their faith together—in families and congregations, as well as in small groups of friends at schools and campuses. John Wesley called this practice,

Soul Tending: Life-Forming Practices for Older Youth & Young Adults

"Christian conferencing," where Christians form communities that "watch over each other in love" and support one another in the life of faith.

In an earlier book, *The Godbearing Life*, we sought to lay out a model for spiritual formation among young people that relied less on gimmickry and programmatic pizzazz and much more, instead, on the historic practices of faith of the Christian community. SOUL TENDING continues this conversation and broadens the invitation to explore practices of faith with youth as the primary curriculum for their spiritual formation. Where we tried to offer a sampler appetizer plate with just a handful of Christian practices, SOUL TENDING lays out a full buffet of forty-three individual and communal practices (from the perspective of thirteen different authors) that have the power and potential to form mature faith in teenagers and adults alike. With a healthy balance between faithful instruction (information) and soulful experience (formation), SOUL TENDING serves as a primer in spirituality in the best sense of the word.

> Christian practices help us loosen our grip on the wrong things so we can reach toward the right things. They till the soul-soil, knead the clay, and loosen our knotted lives a little.

A note of caution: Practices don't transform us. God transforms us. Christian practices help us loosen our grip on the wrong things so we can reach toward the right things. They till the soul-soil, knead the clay, and loosen our knotted lives a little. When we "practice" our faith, we make room for the Holy Spirit to blow through our lives more freely, allowing ourselves to be invaded by God's grace, which is what makes imitating Christ possible in the first place. Our prayer is that the practices contained within this book and the gracious God who is always there first, long before we show up, might offer you an entrance for the holy.

—Kenda Creasy Dean and Ron Foster

Kenda Creasy Dean and her husband Kevin are gladly tending the souls of their two children, Brendan (who is old enough to tend his own) and Shannon (who just thinks she is). An ordained elder in the Baltimore-Washington Annual Conference of The United Methodist Church and a graduate of Wesley Theological Seminary, Kenda serves as assistant professor of youth, church, and culture at Princeton Theological Seminary. Her books include *The Godbearing Life: The Art of Soul Tending for Youth Ministry* (co-authored with Ron Foster), *Starting Right: Thinking Theologically about Youth Ministry* (with Chap Clark and Dave Rahn), and *Practicing Passion: The Adolescent Search for a Passionate Church* (forthcoming).

Ron Foster is the adoring father of two daughters, Christine and Sara, and along with his wife, Holly, and cocker spaniels, Rex and Buddy, resides in Rockville, Maryland. Foster has worked with youth in churches for nearly twenty years as a volunteer, retreat speaker, bike camp director, mission trip leader, and pastor. Ron co-authored *The Godbearing Life: The Art of Soul Tending for Youth Ministry* with Kenda Creasy Dean. He has been a regular instructor at the Princeton Theological Seminary Youth Ministry Institute helping to train others who have a passion for youth ministry. When he's not playing pick-up basketball, Ron spends his time serving as the pastor of Bethesda United Methodist Church.

Introduction

A Spiritual Formation Journey

The Fast Track

It was a hard wall to hit, and it came out of nowhere—or so I thought. Since my early years in high school, I had been on a spiritual "fast track." I preached my first sermon at the age of fifteen. I served on several committees in my local church. In my junior and senior years, I was president of the church youth group. After a brief period of vocational struggle, I went to college where I majored in youth ministry. I began my first full-time youth ministry job at the age of twenty. Then at twenty-two, I moved to a larger church and began seminary. My life, my spiritual journey, and my career were all on "overdrive." Then came the wall.

> The question came out of nowhere and pierced the deafening silence of my spiritual life: "How is it with your soul?" she asked.

The Wall

Trying to keep pace on this fast track left me completely exhausted and on the verge of burnout. For years I had been living out my faith in a subconscious attempt to achieve "super-Christian" status. For me, it was an effort to earn the love and acceptance of God when I was struggling to love myself. I believed that trying harder, doing more, learning more, and teaching more would eventually get me the love I craved and fill my inner longing. I would finally be the person that God wanted me to be.

Of course, I taught just the opposite. I preached of a loving God in Jesus Christ who accepts us where we are. Yet I lived as if I were a kindergartner earning stickers for significant milestones or a football player earning decals for great plays. I had gold stars from sermons that I preached, degrees that I received, and youth whom I had helped. I was trying to become a "superstar" of the spiritual life in order to earn God's love.

The warning signs had been flashing for months. My prayer life had become virtually non-existent. The only time I opened my Bible was to prepare for a lesson or a sermon. My time and energy at work were spent on creating activities to draw kids into the church. Worst of all, I felt like I was leading young people into our *program* instead of into a life-transforming *relationship* with the risen Christ. By all accounts, I was well on my way to reaching "superstar" status. People encouraged me to "reach for the stars" and congratulated me each time I climbed another rung on the spiritual ladder. Pretty soon, my ego outweighed my faith, but I was the only one who knew that. The outward signs of my faith remained shiny and strong, yet my well was dry and the wall was hard.

The Question

The question came out of nowhere and pierced the deafening silence of my spiritual life: "How is it with your soul?" she asked. Julie was a high school junior who consistently attended our youth group events and activities. She was quiet, slightly withdrawn, and very awkward around other people. She was one of those students with whom I never seemed to connect—until that night.

She pressed on, "You always ask us that question. I just wasn't sure if anyone ever asked you, so I thought I would. I just wanted you to know that I care." Stumbling, I answered her question. But by looking into her eyes, I knew I wasn't fooling her. Soon, everyone went home. I went to my car and started the engine. When the parking lot was empty, the tears came easily. I knew that my spiritual life had been dry for months, but now so did someone else.

A Turning Point

In an effort to "jump start" my spiritual life, I attended a retreat designed for adults in youth ministry to help me develop spiritual practices. At the outset, I was looking for a quick fix to an enduring problem. I wanted to be able to go home and give Julie an answer to her question. But somewhere, in the stillness of a morning walk on a mountain path, God showed up.

That morning I read from the Gospel of John where Jesus called his first disciples. John was sitting by the side of the road with a couple of his disciples when Jesus passed by. John saw Jesus coming and pointed him out to his disciples, "Look, the Lamb of God!" The disciples turned and immediately followed Jesus.

On that mountain path, I realized that I was overwhelmed by the exhaustion of "pointing" to Jesus. The problem was, unlike John, I would not have been able to recognize Jesus if he passed by. I had gotten so busy trying to point Jesus out to others that I became disconnected from the Jesus who longed to be in relationship with me. The longing of my heart was to know Christ, yet the work of my life was to keep up my outward appearances for others while trying to earn the love of God.

That weekend was a turning point in my spiritual journey. I realized that in order to be effective in the ministry to which I had been called, I needed to be in an authentic relationship with Jesus

Soul Tending: Life-Forming Practices for Older Youth & Young Adults

Christ. For me, renewing my relationship with Jesus began with accepting God's grace and realizing that God loved me for who I was, not for what I did. My relationship with Christ was freed from the burden of an achievement-oriented faith, and I was able to see myself through Jesus' eyes: a beloved child of God. With that perspective, I realized I needed to "return to my first love" and recapture the passion for my faith that I once held dear.

I needed to fall in love with Christ and connect to him through spiritual practices and an authentic pursuit of a holy life. I also realized that this change would not be a quick fix. It needed to be a long-term transformation in the way I viewed my spiritual life. My soul was burned out and could not be kept ablaze with anything but the light of Christ.

My deep longing could only be filled by coming into the presence of the Almighty and drinking from the well of life. I needed to "sit at the feet" of the saints—some young and some old—to learn practices of the Christian faith that could help me connect with God. I needed to submit myself to a lifelong journey of spiritual formation.

> My deep longing could only be filled by coming into the presence of the Almighty and drinking from the well of life.

The Longing

The yearning of my soul was in accord with so many young people of Generation X and the Millennial generation. We yearn to be a part of something that is greater than ourselves. We want to commit to something worthy of our undying allegiance.

You only need to turn on the TV or the radio to identify these pervasive desires. You find the same story on every show: Young people moving in and out of dating relationships, friendships, and jobs, searching for spiritual connection. TV characters attempting to fill their voids with "committed relationships" that last for less than a season or with sexual encounters that last for a single segment lure us. In the movies, we watch young people search for meaning at fraternity parties or in shallow friendships. We hear the angst of young people, who look behind all of the wrong doors, in songs that cry out for love, attention, and acceptance.

Today's television shows, movies, and songs draw our attention, not only for their entertainment value, but also because we want to see if the seekers there can find what they are looking for: spiritual connection and meaning for their lives. We connect easily with other people who seek the same things we seek; and we watch and listen, expectant that someone will find the answers.

This longing is also evident in Christian culture. Recently, I spoke at a youth camp. One of the songs we sang there, "In the Secret," captured our passions and gave voice for this longing for authentic connection with God. Its lyrics speak of God's being in the secret and quiet places. The lyricist writes of longing to know God, to see

God's face, to touch God, and to hear God's voice. Indeed, we are a generation desperate to know God, to enter into a loving relationship with the Creator, and to experience the grace of God's touch in our lives.

On the soul tending journey, our ultimate desire is for our lives with God to "catch fire" in such a way that we can set ablaze the spiritual lives of others. The challenge is to move beyond our traditional understanding of "being Christian" and enter together, young and old, into a journey with life-forming practices that can help us truly experience God's grace and get fired up for God.

A Birthday Lesson

In my house growing up, you were only allowed to light a fire in the fireplace if you were ten years old or older. I'll never forget my tenth birthday. I had been waiting for that day for years, watching all three of my older brothers enjoy the enviable task of fire-starting and knowing that I could do it better.

On the night of my tenth birthday, we all gathered in the living room to watch my first fire. I crumpled up a whole Sunday newspaper and lined the bottom of the fireplace. I placed a few logs on top of the pile of newspapers and lit the fire. We turned out the lights and I, as a proud inventor, watched the fire burn brighter than any my family had ever seen—for about ninety seconds. Then the fire faded, and the room got darker; so I threw some more newspaper in. For forty-five minutes, I repeated the process until three weeks of Sunday papers were gone, and the logs were still unscathed. My oldest brother, David, helped me see that I had spent so much time focusing on getting the fire started that I never thought about how to keep it going.

A Fading Fire

Sometimes our faith falls into the same trap. We experience God's amazing grace at a retreat or a camp, and we commit to living our lives for Christ. Soon after the experience (or the newspaper) burns out of our memory, the fire begins to fade. Then, we search for the next experience (or newspaper) to help get us started again.

Our spiritual lives become a continual process of seeking, yet we end up chasing after "newspapers" instead of "logs" that can fuel the fires of our soul for a lifetime journey with Christ.

The Invitation

Where can you find those logs to start and feed a roaring blaze in your soul, filling your heart's deepest longing? You'll find them on a "soul tending" journey, where you'll experience authentic life-transforming encounters with God's grace.

You are invited to tend the fire of your faith, so that you will burn brightly with the love of Jesus Christ now and for years to come.

Millions of people—who have longed for God just as you and I do—have traveled this journey for thousands of years. Although full of ancient mystery, this adventure amazingly applies to modern seekers' lives. Join this journey, youth and young adults alike, and discover the fire of the Holy Spirit from which you can recharge your soul and find new life. Young seeker, tend your soul's fire and satisfy your heart's yearning with the real presence of God.

> You are invited to tend the fire of your faith, so that you will burn brightly with the love of Jesus Christ now and for years to come.

Is This Journey for You?

Are you ready for the trip? Answer these questions to determine if you're prepared to tend your soul's fire:

❖ Is your spiritual life dominated by a search for the next big event (or the "newspaper") to light your soul's fire, but you want to find the "logs" needed to sustain the blaze?

❖ Is your heart's cry to know Christ more deeply?

❖ Are you ready to submit yourself to a journey through the Christian practices that can lead to authentic transformation and an intimate connection with the Creator?

If you answered yes to any of these questions, then this invitation is indeed for you! Embrace the Christian practices; they will fuel your heart's fire and keep your spirit burning for years to come.

The Warnings

Your trip won't be easy. Fatigue, discomfort, and frustration may tempt you to give up your itinerary, but I urge you to keep at it. Some distractions may cause you to lose focus. Stay on guard for these:

❖ **Unrealistic expectations**
Using this book won't help you master the Christian faith and its practices. In fact, as Kenda Creasy Dean and Ron Foster point out in their book, *The Godbearing Life*, "We do not master [spiritual] practices; practices master us."[1] Rather, this book will aid you along the way through a lifelong journey of spiritual formation. Paul writes to the churches in Galatia that he yearns to see Christ formed in them (see Galatians 4:19). The essence of spiritual formation is that our lives are shaped and molded until they begin to take on the form of Jesus Christ.

❖ **An incomplete journey**
Using this resource from beginning to end will not complete your spiritual formation. From this introduction to spiritual practices, you will need to determine which of the practices to

make your own. This resource will help you try them on, stretch them out, and experience them so that you can build habits that will shape your journey for years to come. Choose carefully with your goal in mind: to have Christ formed in you. Remember that participating in these spiritual practices is not a matter of trying to *earn* God's love. Rather, the practices will *train you* to live out the way of Christ in your daily life. Don't fall into the trap of doing this study to climb up another rung on a spiritual ladder. If you submit yourself to this experience of an authentic journey with the living God, *your life will be changed*.

❖ A mechanical prescription for a holy life

You may be tempted to see the Christian practices as a mechanical prescription for achieving a "holy life." John Wesley called this danger *formalism*, which means replacing a life-transforming relationship with God in Jesus Christ with "keeping church."

This trap is the one with which I have most struggled. It is easy for me to fall into the trap of "keeping church" by doing all of the *outward* things (including spiritual practices) that are expected of Christians without allowing those things to transform and shape my *inner* life.

For this soul-tending journey to be of lasting value, you must allow the deepest parts of your soul to be exposed to the transforming work of Jesus Christ. You must not allow the practices to become *outward* signs of an *outward* faith that lead to an *outward* righteousness. Instead, they must become *outward* signs of an *inward* grace working in your life to transform you into the image and likeness of Christ on the inside, on the outside, and in relationship with others.

The Practices

When I was attempting to learn to play the guitar, I bought three different books on the skill for "beginners" and "dummies." I got a great guitar and all of the appropriate equipment and accessories. I practiced the exercises hundreds of times, trying to master the chords and progressions. But after a few months' work, my family was practically begging me to give it up—so I did.

After hearing my story, my young friend said that my main mistake was that I never actually *played*, I *just* practiced. What I should have done, according to this wise, young friend, was turned on the radio or sat with an experienced guitarist and just played along until eventually the sounds blended as one. What he meant was that we cannot do things in isolation, expecting them to miraculously become woven into the fabric and context of our lives.

Soul Tending: Life-Forming Practices for Older Youth & Young Adults

You learn the alphabet letter by letter. While memorizing the alphabet is a good skill to possess, it won't get you very far unless you put the letters together as you read and write.

The same holds true for the Christian faith. Like chords and letters, spiritual practices help us *learn how to,* in this case, live a life of faith. But they are more than a tool. They are also the means by which we *actually live* a life of faith. Christian practices help bring our lives and the life of Christ into a beautiful harmony.

Just as you can't play an instrument or learn to read without practice, you can't live a life of faith without doing the spiritual practices. However, if you do the spiritual practices outside the context of a life of faith, you engage in empty ritual. Through these practices, "God wants to restore in each of us the image of God so that love will govern our hearts and lives and begin to heal our relationships with God, neighbor, and creation."[2]

The Means of Grace

God, through Jesus Christ, has offered to each of us an amazing gift of love that we can never earn and we do not deserve. We call this *grace*—the free gift of God's love poured out in Jesus Christ. Christian practices are a way or means of receiving that grace into our lives.

> The practices of soul tending put us in a place to be transformed by that gift of grace.

Another way to look at this is that the Christian practices put us in the way of grace. They do not help us earn God's grace, which would be an impossible task because grace is free. Rather, the practices of soul tending put us in a place to be transformed by that gift of grace. God uses these means of grace to strengthen God's children and the church for the task of living faithfully as disciples. Christian practices mark us as Christ's disciples and make us into faithful followers formed in the image and likeness of Christ.

What Does the Journey Look Like?

In their book *The Godbearing Life*, Kenda Creasy Dean and Ron Foster point to five essential characteristics of a soul-tending journey with the Christian practices:

1. Spiritual practices require active participation.

My young, guitar-playing friend taught me this very important lesson. The only way to experience the fullness of God's grace available through the practices of faith is to *do* them. This understanding does not mean that we use this book as a quick recipe for spiritual holiness—moving from practice to practice until we have "done" them all. However, we are invited to experience the practices, to live with them, to work at them as Christ is formed in us. In order to experience the practices as a means of grace, we must faithfully commit to doing them.

2. Christian practices do something to us.

By submitting ourselves to the Christian practices, we open our lives to be shaped and transformed into the image of Christ. This vulnerability to be shaped and transformed involves an often-difficult process of letting go of control over our own lives and allowing God to shape us. We do not use the practices of faith to achieve something. God uses the practices as a way to work in our lives to form Christ in us—to make us holy as Christ is holy. We must never see ourselves as the *subjects* in the journey of spiritual formation. We are the *objects* who receive the grace of God through our participation in the spiritual practices. Marjorie Thompson says in *Soul Feast* that we must be clear that "Christian spirituality begins with God, depends on God, and ends in God."[3] Spiritual practice is God's way of pouring out grace on our lives and love into our hearts.

3. The practices involve other people who "do faith" with us.

This soul tending journey is not one that we can do alone. Most of us are comfortable being in community with others where our togetherness is based on common characteristics, interests, and history. We understand what it means to be together with people who are like us or are a part of "our" church or youth group. But comfortable relationships are not the full extent of what God intends for people of faith.

Rather, we are called to be in *communion* with others in the body of Christ. Being in communion with others on this journey means that "we participate in a common life, united by Jesus Christ, not by mutual interests or similar personalities, and experience the joys and pains of others as though they were our own."[4] To be a part of a communion requires being willing to forgive one another, to trust one another, to bear one another's burdens, and to defer our own interests to the interests of others. Real intimacy happens when we are willing to journey with others in love and practice the faith together.

One of the essentials of true communion is that people of all ages join together, united in Christ. The soul tending journey is not one for experts and learners. It is a journey where people of all ages are invited to walk together, grow together, and learn together. We do not intend this book to be taught by an adult leader to a group of student learners. Instead, we invite youth, young adults, and adults to travel as co-journers, hand-in-hand and side-by-side.

You will learn from and teach one another. Wisdom will come from age and experience, and sometimes it will come through the keen insight of the young. When I have been willing to risk being a co-journer with others, I have been taught by fifteen and sixteen-year-old saints, as well as by those who are my elders.

4. Christian practices are the continuation of an ancient tradition.

This book is not the first attempt to record practices that will help people on the journey of faith, and it will not be the last. Christian practices have been around for ages. By experiencing the practices, we become part of the continually unfolding love story of God's relationship with God's children.

The Hebrew people stood at the mouth of the Red Sea and prayed for deliverance. Daniel searched the Scriptures to find wisdom and strength to stand against Nebuchadnezzar. Mary and Martha broke bread in communion with Jesus. Jesus himself sought times to be alone with his heavenly Father. Through the centuries since Jesus' ministry, people of all ages and in all times have practiced their faith. Saint Augustine connected with God through sometimes desperate prayers. John and Charles Wesley were accountable to each other as members of the Holy Club at Oxford. Mother Teresa saw Christ in every person she encountered as she reached out in love to the "least of these." As we participate in these ancient Christian practices, we become part of this story. Our lives are bound together with those who have gone before us and those who will come after us.

5. Finally, Christian practices call for a standard of excellence.

This does not mean that we will ever be able to perfect the practices and earn our stripes as spiritual giants. However, it does mean that we must commit to practicing the faith in the same way a runner prepares for a marathon. As in training for a sport, we cannot give meager amounts of time and energy to practicing the faith and expect to have our lives "in shape." We must offer God our best, knowing that even our most valiant attempts will fall short. Paul reminds us that God's power is made perfect in our weakness (2 Corinthians 12:8-9). If we offer God our best, God can transform those feeble efforts into beautiful works of art.

At the same time, we must recognize that we will not start as experts. People who have been practicing the faith for years still have their minds wander during periods of solitude or fall asleep while listening to a prayer. Do not get discouraged. Jump in and allow God's grace to work in you as you grow in faith and are formed into the image of Christ.

The Beginning

Expanding on the ideas put forth by Kenda Creasy Dean and Ron Foster in *The Godbearing Life*, this book will help you study the practices, but most importantly it will guide you in living out these holy habits through which God freely pours out grace upon grace.

As you begin your journey with the Christian practices, I encourage you to seek out people whose bold and passionate commitments to Jesus Christ are evidenced in how they live. Think of people whose burning faith for Jesus gives light all around them. They may be family members, friends, congregation members, pastors, or youth workers—youth or adults. Sit at their feet, learning what spiritual formation practices they have found helpful on their journeys. Listen to their stories and soak up their wisdom.

Hopefully, your journey will be filled with tremendous growth, incredibly transforming your spiritual life. My prayer is that you will draw near to Jesus; that these practices will open to you God's grace; and most importantly, that this step would be the beginning of a lifelong journey that leads to Christ's "being formed in you."

Notes

[1] Reprinted from *The Godbearing Life: The Art of Soul Tending for Youth Ministry* by Kenda Creasy Dean and Ron Foster. © Copyright 1998 by Kenda Creasy Dean and Ron Foster (Upper Room Books: Nashville). Used by permission.

[2] Reprinted from *Eight Life-Enriching Practices of United Methodists* by Henry H. Knight III, ©2001 Abingdon Press, All rights reserved. Used by permission.

[3] Reprinted from *Soul Feast: An Invitation to the Christian Spiritual Life* by Marjorie J. Thompson. ©1995 by Marjorie J. Thompson. Used by permission.

[4] Reprinted from *The Godbearing Life*.

Discussion Guide for "A Spiritual Formation Journey"

❖ What is your faith story? At what points, if any, did you feel any connections to the writer's faith story?

❖ The writer tells about a time when he tried everything to convince others and himself that he was close to God. In what ways have you struggled to earn God's love?

❖ Where do you see the longing for God in today's culture?

❖ What experiences of being "on fire" for God have you had? Have you encountered the same kind of faith burnout of which the writer speaks?

❖ What is the difference between knowing *how to live* a life of faith and *living* a life of faith?

❖ What are ways to tend the fires of our souls?

❖ What life-forming practices are already a part of your soul tending journey?

❖ What are the five characteristics of a soul tending journey with the Christian practices? What are the warnings?

❖ How can the faith community help on a spiritual journey?

Discuss your answers and any thoughts about the following questions from the text:

❖ Is your spiritual life dominated by a search for the next big event ("newspapers") to light your soul's fire, but you want to find the "logs" needed to sustain the blaze?

❖ Is your heart's cry to know Christ more deeply?

❖ Are you ready to submit yourself to a journey through the Christian practices that can lead to authentic transformation and an intimate connection with the Creator?

Tending In

Tiger Woods knows golf. He is the master of his craft and is quickly becoming the greatest player of all time. I, on the other hand, have not mastered the sport. I do my best to keep up the appearance of a professional golfer. Like millions of other golfers, I buy clothes, golf balls, clubs, hats, and other "golf gimmicks" endorsed by Tiger Woods. I hope that by looking like a pro, I will play like a pro. In my skateboarding days, we would call someone like that a "poser"—the person looked the part but couldn't live it. The difference between Tiger Woods and me is clear: I have the game "on," but he has the game "in" him.

For many years, that is how I understood the Christian life. I did my best to put the game on. I kept up appearances by doing all of the things a Christian was supposed to do: go to church, lead the youth group, pray in public, even share my faith with others. By all accounts, the masks I wore were doing their jobs. The problem was that all of the outward signs of my life with Christ were not paired with the inward realities of a transformed life.

The first act of soul tending is to open ourselves for an inward soul transformation. When we "tend in," we tend the soul fires, which are not available for public examination.

In order to tend the fire of his own soul, Jesus knew that he needed to pull apart from the crowds that followed him and the disciples who walked with him in order to spend time with his heavenly Father. In the midst of the busyness of his life and ministry, Jesus sought a spiritual connection with God. Scripture says, "As often as possible Jesus withdrew to out-of-the-way places for prayer" (Luke 5:15-16, *Message*).

In the same way, as demands of school, jobs, family commitments, and ministry crowd in on our lives, we need to "withdraw" from the clutter to find the Christ. Inward practices will give you the tools to tend your soul as you, too, seek still, quiet places to meet your heavenly Father.

As you carve out time and space to encounter Jesus, you will meet an amazing love that will welcome, affirm, challenge, and help you to grow. As your soul draws near to Christ through these practices, you will develop life patterns that train you to think and act like Christ, becoming his hands and feet for those around you. Your inner transformation will flow from your soul into your body, into your relationships, and into your world.

> As your soul draws near to Christ through these practices, you will develop life patterns that train you to think and act like Christ, becoming his hands and feet for those around you.

Meditation

 ## igns of the Spirit

Discuss where you have seen God's Spirit at work this week. How have you experienced grace in a new way through Christian practice? Discuss any joys or struggles you had. How is it with your soul?

 ## urpose

Because we long for Christ to be formed in us, we make this covenant to tend the fires of our souls so that our longing for Christ may never be extinguished and that our lives will be set ablaze with his love.

 ## nstruction

Think about the word *meditation* and answer these questions:

❖ What are the first images that come to your mind when you hear the word?

❖ Have you heard the word used before? If so, in what context?

❖ Have you ever meditated on anything?

The Gift of Meditation

When we think of meditation, sometimes we get the image of a monk or holy person chanting and sitting in a trance with crossed legs, surrounded by candles and incense. The practice is often associated with Buddhism; however, meditation is also a tool for discipleship in our Christian walk. Meditation is a spiritual discipline that lies at the heart of the context of our faith as followers of Christ. Meditation can also mean contemplation, pondering, thoughtful reflection, and imagery. Meditation is linked closely to prayer because meditation is a form of prayer. When we meditate, we clear our minds and let God do the talking. Meditation is a gift from God that allows us a closer communion with our Creator, Redeemer, and Sustainer.

❖ When you hear the word *communion*, what comes to mind?

❖ When you pray, who talks and who listens?

> "It's nice to be at peace
> with you. It's fine with
> me to be close to you."
> — "Peace with You,"
> from *Breathe*
> by Ten Shekel Shirt[1]

What Is Meditation?

Meditation involves the use of a particular image or verse from the biblical text to focus our hearts and minds on the presence of God in our midst. Through meditation, we allow the time and space to let God consume our thoughts until God's words are our words.

Recite aloud together the verse from Psalm 119. The people of Israel understood the importance of taking the time to listen to the Word of God through the reading and hearing of the Law or Torah. You may have even participated in something called a guided meditation where a story or a biblical passage is read by a group leader who invites you to focus on a particular area of your faith. Meditation involves a physical stillness and silence accompanied by an emptying of the mind to allow, what the Trappist monk Thomas Merton called, the echo of God to resonate through us.

How Do We Practice Meditation?

Meditation is not confined to chunks of time we take out of our schedules. It can also be the state of mind in which we actively experience life in the midst of our busyness. As we live our daily lives, we can contemplate or meditate continuously on some thought or image in our minds. Have you ever had a song or jingle stuck in your head?

Meditation as a state of mind is very similar (except not so annoying). Words or images from the Scriptures get "stuck" in your mind. You are left repeating them continually throughout the day, offering you a more peaceful and prayerful approach to your sometimes hectic life. However you practice meditation, it, like prayer, frees up time out of your busy schedule to be in communion with God. We rest our voices and still our hearts and minds to listen for God's voice in our lives. The practice of meditation or contemplation offers us the kind of peace talked about in the line from the song by Ten Shekel Shirt. It is the kind of peace we find only when we are in the presence of God, and we know we are fine.

 ehearsal

Choose a simple phrase, such as *God is good*, upon which to meditate. Allow some silence for each of you to consider God's goodness. Then, take some time in the quiet to think about how good God has been to you. Listen to what God might be saying to you about God's goodness. After a few minutes have passed, offer an "amen" and debrief the experience.

> I will meditate on your precepts, and fix my eyes on your ways.
> —Psalm 119:15

 nvolving

What kind of ripples might (or have) come about from practicing meditation? How could your daily routine change by the transformation taking place in your soul? Discuss how you might see all areas of your life—home, school, nature, community, world, job, paying bills, and so forth—connected in a new way based on your spiritual formation journey.

 omorrow

❑ Commit to thirty minutes each day this week to spend in meditation.

❑ Choose a life situation you are facing on which to contemplate. Keep a journal to write about your experiences.

❑ Memorize a phrase, a Scripture, a song, and so forth to weave into your thoughts for a week. Listen for God's voice as you play the phrase over and over in your heart.

Notes
[1] ©2000 Integrity's Hosanna! Music/ASCAP
c/o Integrity Music, Inc., 1000 Cody Road, Mobile, AL 36695

Stillness and Silence

 **igns of the Spirit**

Discuss where you have seen God's Spirit at work this week. How have you experienced grace in a new way through Christian practice? Discuss any joys or struggles you had. How is it with your soul?

 **urpose**

Because we long for Christ to be formed in us, we make this covenant to tend the fires of our souls so that our longing for Christ may never be extinguished and that our lives will be set ablaze with his love.

 **nstruction**

The Dividends of Silence

Food is satisfying. We feel its effects in a full stomach, increased energy, and improved mental focus. We expect to eat three meals a day plus snacks. None of us likes to go too long without a bite to eat, something to fill ourselves up. Think of a time when you were really hungry. How did you feel when you finally got to eat?

Spiritual writer Morton Kelsey compares our physical need for food with our spiritual need for silence. He says that as the body needs regular intake of food to sustain health, the soul needs regular periods of silence in order to thrive.

Write your thoughts on these questions:

❖ How long could you survive without food?

> For God alone my soul waits in silence for my hope is from him. He alone is my rock and my salvation, my fortress; I shall not be shaken. On God rests my deliverance and my honor; my mighty rock, my refuge is in God.
> —Psalm 62:5-7

❖ How long could you survive without silence?

❖ When do you have periods of silence in your life?

❖ Are you comfortable with silence? Why or why not?

Silence Scares Me!

Silence can be frightening. One young person said, "I don't know what to do with silence. I always have music or the television on, even if I'm alone and have no one to talk to." Does this sound familiar?

❖ Why do you think we are uncomfortable with silence?

❖ Have you ever had a time when you enjoyed silence?

Our world is filled with sounds. We are rarely in total silence. Writer Dallas Willard challenges his readers to consider their inner emptiness if they must always surround themselves with noise. Take the time right now to sit absolutely quiet for one minute and discover what you hear when your voice is silent. Discuss:

❖ What sounds did you hear?

❖ Would you have paid attention to those sounds if they were in the background of conversation?

❖ What were you thinking about during the silence?

God Can Be in the Silence

Select someone to read aloud the story of how Elijah met God at Horeb. This passage occurs when the prophet Elijah ran away because Queen Jezebel threatened to kill him. Elijah is discouraged and wants to die because he feels his life's work is a failure. Read 1 Kings 19:11-15 to see what happens next.

The Lord was not in the wind. The Lord was not in the earthquake. The Lord was not in the fire. When Elijah finally faced the "sheer silence" or "still, small voice," he could hear God. What does this story say to you?

Befriending the Silence

For centuries the breath prayer has existed as a way to connect with God. For some it is a way to befriend the silence; it gives you something to do as you begin to experience holy silence. As you repeat the prayer, its words eventually become background so you can be open to hearing what God might say. You can choose your own breath prayer and then repeat it over and over in rhythm with the inhale and exhale of your breath. First, choose a simple phrase that summarizes what you may need from your relationship with God right now. You might choose a line from a song or a phrase of Scripture, as long as it is not too wordy. (You want to fit all the words on your inhale and exhale, and you don't want to hyperventilate!) Or you could use something like, "Be with me, God"; "Jesus, help me follow you"; "Spirit, give me strength"; "Gracious God, fill me with love"; or "Guide me, Savior."

 ehearsal

Think of a prayer that you will use or select one from above. Sit with bodies stilled and palms upturned on knees to spend time in silence. Breathe deeply in and out as you begin to breathe your prayer to God. After three to five minutes, close the silence with an "amen." Discuss what the experience was like.

Play some peaceful music and try to sit in stillness to listen. Since most of us are used to being physically active, this may be challenging! Close your eyes to better concentrate on being still. Sit absolutely still without moving a muscle and become aware first of physical stillness. Then, move your focus onto your inward stillness. When the song ends, talk about what it felt like to be absolutely still.

 nvolving

What kind of ripples might (or have) come about from practicing stillness and silence? How could your daily routine change by the transformation taking place in your soul? Discuss how you might see all areas of your life—home, school, nature, community, world, job, paying bills, and so forth—connected in a new way based on your spiritual formation journey.

 omorrow

❑ Take a silent walk by yourself through your neighborhood. Use this as a time of meditation, of opening yourself to God. Try to use all of your senses to appreciate the beauty of creation around you.

❑ Find a place where you can be by yourself in silence. Read Isaiah 43:1-5a, substituting your own name for "O Jacob" in verse one. Get comfortable and take a few deep breaths. Then read the personalized verses from Isaiah over and over, slowly. Try to picture yourself resting in God's hands or loving embrace. Imagine that God is speaking these words directly to you.

❑ Designate a period of time when you will "fast from words." You may not be totally able to remain silent but see if you can focus on staying as quiet as possible. If you must speak, choose your words carefully. Remember these words from Ecclesiastes 5:2: "Never be rash with your mouth, nor let your heart be quick to utter a word before God, for God is in heaven, and you upon earth; therefore let your words be few."

❑ Find a place where you can be still by yourself in silence. Set a timer for five minutes, then close your eyes, sit up straight, and relax into the silence. You might want to begin with a prayer like, "O God, be with me now." Don't try to make anything happen. When distracting thoughts come, refocus on the silence or repeat the prayer.

❑ Make time to pray your breath prayer. You could designate certain times of day (for example, when you awaken and just before you go to sleep), or certain actions (for example, every time you brush your teeth), or an amount of time (for example, set a timer for two minutes).

Discernment

Signs of the Spirit

Discuss where you have seen God's Spirit at work this week. How have you experienced grace in a new way through Christian practice? Discuss any joys or struggles you had. How is it with your soul?

Purpose

Because we long for Christ to be formed in us, we make this covenant to tend the fires of our souls so that our longing for Christ may never be extinguished and that our lives will be set ablaze with his love.

Instruction

Each of us is called upon to make numerous decisions every day of our lives. Some decisions are easy: What do I wear today? Do I raise my hand to answer the teacher's question? Others are harder: Do I tell my best friend I am angry at her? Do I break up with my boyfriend or girlfriend? How we make our decisions says a lot about who we are and about our relationship with God.

> I call heaven and earth to witness against you today that I have set before you life and death, blessings and curses. Choose life so that you and your descendants may live.
>
> —Deuteronomy 30:19

Choices, Choices

Would you choose pizza or pancakes? vanilla or chocolate? punk rock or hip-hop? love or hate? to live in Alaska or Florida? wealth or popularity? popularity or faithfulness to God? college or work? life or death? Discuss which choices were easy to make. Which were hard? Why? In pairs, talk about a difficult choice each of you has made in the past year.

Tools for the Task

What are some of the tools you use when you have to make a difficult decision? Be sure to include in your decision-making tool box the following: Think through the pros and cons; talk with a family member, friend, or spiritual director; pray or journal about the decision; use the process of discernment.

What Is Discernment?

We can make most of our choices by ourselves, but sometimes a decision seems complicated and we know we need God's help.

Many choices will come easily out of who we understand ourselves to be. As a person of faith, I will not spread rumors, tell lies, or abuse my body. Yet what do I do about being in a relationship with a friend who encourages me to do those things? How do I know which college will be the best fit for me? How do I know when I'm ready to get married? How do I choose between activities I love when there is not time to do everything?

Making Decisions With God's Help

Discernment is the process of making decisions with God's help. Centuries ago, Ignatius of Loyola suggested a "process of discernment" to guide people of faith through their decision-making. Here's a simple way to follow Ignatius' ideas:

❖ Gather all the information you need in order to make a particular decision. This may include talking to persons who would have helpful insight into your situation or friends who know you well.

❖ Focus on one choice for a specific period of time. Write down all the reasons that support this option. Pray about it. Try to live as though you have made this choice, then pay attention to how you feel with this choice. Next spend the same amount of time living with and praying about the other choice. How do you feel with your options now?

❖ Make a tentative decision after considering your feelings with all possible choices. Do you feel more peaceful with one decision? If so, offer that decision to God and know that you made the best possible decision you could make. If you still feel troubled about the decision, try the alternative choice or postpone the decision, if possible.

Prayerful Decision-Making

Discernment is a way of making decisions that reminds us we are not alone. God undergirds us in all that we do, and we have other people who can support us as we wrestle through complicated or troubling decisions. Look to the example of Jesus and other biblical figures to see how they made choices. In all our decisions, large and small, we can raise these questions with ourselves:

❖ Is this choice consistent with who God calls me to be?
❖ Is the Holy Spirit informing this decision?
❖ Which choice will help me become a more complete person?
❖ After spending quiet time with God about this decision, do I feel a leaning toward one alternative?

ehearsal

What are some of the hardest decisions you make? What resources are available to help you make decisions?

Make a list of questions the persons below could consider in the discernment process. How could they make the right decision? Who might each of these young people enlist as helpers in the process?

❖ Maria is sixteen, pregnant, and must decide what to do for her future: Keep the baby, have an abortion, or give the child up for adoption.
❖ Sam's mother's new job means a move to another state. Sam would like to stay in his current town to finish his last year of high school but doesn't want to be separated from his family.
❖ Anissa has been offered a job that might help her toward a future career. Taking the job, however, would mean she'd work on Sundays, so she would miss worship and church activities.

> If we live by the Spirit, let us also be guided by the Spirit.
> —Galatians 5:25

None of us knows what decisions we will be called upon to make in the future; but as followers of Jesus, we do know certain things about ourselves. Think about the statements below. Which ones can you claim in your own life? If one doesn't sound right for you, think about why you can't accept its truth.

❖ I am a child of God.
❖ God wants me to be content.
❖ God created me to do good in the world.
❖ I can do all things through Christ who strengthens me.

nvolving

What kind of ripples might (or have) come about from practicing discernment? How could your daily routine change by the transformation taking place in your soul? Discuss how you might see all areas of your life—home, school, nature, community, world, job, paying bills, and so forth—connected in a new way based on your spiritual formation journey.

 omorrow

❑ Talk to your parents or other significant adults in your life about times they have had to make difficult decisions. Find out what process they used. If they don't know about discernment, share what you know with them.

❑ Make a list of decisions you expect to make in the next ten years. How could you begin the discernment process now?

❑ Read the following passages of Scripture every day this week and consider how they apply to prayerful decision-making: Psalm 73:24; Psalm 119:105; Romans 12:2; and James 1:5.

❑ If you are trying to make a decision in your life right now, use the discernment process and spend time talking to God about your options.

Honoring the Body

Signs of the Spirit

Discuss where you have seen God's Spirit at work this week. How have you experienced grace in a new way through Christian practice? Discuss any joys or struggles you had. How is it with your soul?

Purpose

Because we long for Christ to be formed in us, we make this covenant to tend the fires of our souls so that our longing for Christ may never be extinguished and that our lives will be set ablaze with his love.

> Do you not know that you are God's temple and that God's Spirit dwells in you? ... God's temple is holy, and you are that temple.
> —1 Corinthians 3:16, 17b

Instruction

Most of us take our bodies for granted. We don't notice the miracle of our organs and systems until we get sick or injured. Then we may marvel at how the body can heal itself. We inhabit the physical self, our one body/mind/spirit, yet many of us think of ourselves in separate parts. I think (mind), feel and connect to God (spirit), and move or act (body). Yet God made us to be whole selves and called us to physical, spiritual, and mental health.

In Clay Jars

Read aloud 2 Corinthians 4:7-10. Why did Paul use the image of clay jars (or, in other translations, earthen vessels) to describe the human body? What do those images suggest? What are the main points of this passage? What does verse 10 mean? How do we make "the life of Jesus ... visible in our bodies?" Read the quotation from 1 Corinthians 3:16-17b. What does it mean to be the "temple of God"?

Defiling the Temple of God

We don't always carry with us the knowledge that we are "temples of God." We act in ways that harm us, body or soul. Discuss possible ways to honor God in our bodies when it comes to:

- ❖ diet
- ❖ physical activity
- ❖ sexual activity
- ❖ alcohol or drug use
- ❖ smoking cigarettes or using other tobacco substances
- ❖ promoting positive mental health

In what other ways can we honor the body? What are some reasons we sometimes dishonor the body?

The Body/Mind/Spirit Link

Studies show that mental and emotional health is closely linked to physical health. When our physical body is healthy, our spirit is much happier and content. Regular physical activity can help us stay balanced when we experience times of stress.

In pairs talk about what sorts of exercise you enjoy and how you might be able to maintain a regular exercise routine. What would it take for you to love your body? How might you fully grasp that God created you to be a beautiful human being?

Go for Health: My Body Pledge

Each of us can take steps to claim and maintain our own health. We can eat a healthy, balanced diet with lots of fruits and vegetables. We can follow a physical regime that keeps our cardiovascular system strong and our mental state alert. We can abstain from abusing substances that are harmful to us. We can carefully think through all our choices, asking, "Will this help me be healthy? Am I honoring God in me if I do this?"

Write a pledge about how you will honor your body. For example, "I will try to eat five vegetables each day," "I will make an effort to stop smoking," or "I will exercise for thirty minutes three times a week in order to honor my body." Put your pledge in a stamped envelope and address it to yourself. Exchange envelopes with someone and mail the letters in one month as a reminder to check your progress.

 ehearsal

Is "honoring the body" different for younger persons than for adults? Discuss the problems and temptations young people face when it comes to living a healthy lifestyle.

Take a moment to honor one another's body by saying the following affirmation to each group member. Say together, "[Name], you are a child of God. God made you beautiful and you are good."

nvolving

What kind of ripples might (or have) come about from honoring your body? How could your daily routine change by the transformation taking place in your soul? Discuss how you might see all areas of your life—home, school, nature, community, world, job, paying bills, and so forth—connected in a new way based on your spiritual formation journey.

> Or do you not know that your body is a temple of the Holy Spirit within you, which you have from God, and that you are not your own? For you were bought with a price; therefore glorify God in your body.
> —1 Corinthians 6:19-20

omorrow

☐ Keep a food diary for one week, writing down everything you eat. At the end of the week, think about your diet. Is it healthy? How could you commit to healthier eating?

☐ Journal about your relationship to your body. What do you do to stay fit and healthy? Do you see yourself in partnership with the God who made your body? Think about the gift of health. How can you work to stay healthy?

☐ Pray about giving up negative behaviors that keep you away from wholeness and health. Seek support from friends, parents, or a recovery program to battle any addictions.

☐ Meditate on how your emotional and spiritual health are linked to your physical health.

☐ Do online research about a subject that may pertain to your own body experience, for instance, marijuana use, sexually transmitted diseases, eating disorders, or maintaining an exercise regime.

☐ Look straight into a full-length mirror for five minutes each day this week. Observe the wonderful creation God made in you. If you like what you see, thank God. If you do not like what you see, pray that God would show you how special and wonderfully you are made. Talk to a trusted friend or mentor about ways in which you could learn to love and care for your body.

Devotional Reading

 **S**igns of the Spirit

Discuss where you have seen God's Spirit at work this week. How have you experienced grace in a new way through Christian practice? Discuss any joys or struggles you had. How is it with your soul?

 **P**urpose

Because we long for Christ to be formed in us, we make this covenant to tend the fires of our souls so that our longing for Christ may never be extinguished and that our lives will be set ablaze with his love.

 **I**nstruction

The Dream Assignment

Imagine being in school and in the midst of all your reading, homework, and term papers, your teacher hands you a novel with these instructions, "You don't have to finish this book. There will be no report or test. Just find a quiet place, start wherever you like, and read slowly and carefully. When you come across a word, a phrase, or a sentence that is interesting to you, stop and think about it. Do this same thing every day for a week."

> Come before the Lord and begin to read. Stop reading when you feel the Lord drawing you inwardly to himself. Now, simply remain in stillness. Stay there for a while.
> —Jeanne Guyon (1648-1717)

Wow! You could forget about finding the main point, identifying the climax, and labeling the protagonist and antagonist. With that type of assignment, you don't have to worry about diagramming sentences or stress about deadlines.

A Different Kind of Reading

But who really reads like that or has that luxury? In the busyness of our lives, it is much easier to read only as much as needed to get a good grade on the report. It is convenient to skim the newspaper, grabbing the latest headlines on our way out the door. And we surf the Internet with CDs playing in the background or while talking on the phone. Reading is something people do to find specific information or to kill time hoping that something interesting will keep their attention for a few minutes.

Is this how you approach your devotional time? How do you read the Bible or devotional books? Do you have a plan or a method? Are you trying to gain information? to seek answers and guidance? to make you feel better?

Devotional reading allows the Spirit to move and reveal God's love and desire for us. We do not bring a detailed assignment. The Bible is not laid out with flashing headlines to grab our attention, and the highlights are not flashing sound bytes in pop-up windows on the computer screen. Reading spiritually requires a different kind of reading.

Absorbing the Words

Devotional reading provides not only a purpose but also a method. The goal is not to answer who?, what?, when?, where?, and why? The goal in devotional reading is to find God in the words you read. Devotional reading gives you permission to slow down and helps you to truly hear what God has to say specifically through the text. As you read and pray, listen for those things that the Holy Spirit calls to your attention. An influential devotional writer, Madame Guyon, instructs devotional readers to come to the Lord quietly and humbly, absorbing the words on the page.

Discuss:

❖ What books or authors have taught you the most about your relationship with God and with others?

❖ Have you read any of the writings of the saints—ancient or current?

A professor of theology once admitted that as a young adult she thought the whole history of Christianity skipped from Jesus and the apostles to her and her local church. Then she read about the rich history of the church through time and discovered the ancient church mothers, fathers, and saints of the church, like Teresa of Avila and Saint Augustine. She not only increased her knowledge but also found friends and soul mates along her faith journey.

 ehearsal

Choose a selection from a saint of the church or a favorite devotional writer. Say a brief prayer asking the Holy Spirit to reveal God to you in the passage. Read the passage slowly to yourself. You are not skimming for a main point but looking for God. Feel free to stop at a certain word or phrase that speaks to you. Do not panic if your mind wanders. Continue to pray and listen for what God might be speaking to you. The point is not the amount of material you cover but the time you take.

Come back together as a group to discuss your experiences. Was this easy or difficult? Will this take practice? Is this a discipline that you would like to continue? What did you hear God saying to you in the passage?

nvolving

What kind of ripples might (or have) come about from practicing devotional reading? How could your daily routine change by the transformation taking place in your soul? Discuss how you might see all areas of your life—home, school, nature, community, world, job, paying bills, and so forth—connected in a new way based on your spiritual formation journey.

omorrow

❑ Visit *www.methodx.net/connect/* to learn more ways to practice devotional reading. Try some of the guided experiences there for you.

❑ Do some research about a particular saint of the church at a library or on the Internet. Read about him or her and then read his or her writings devotionally.

❑ Commit to reading the same short passage in a devotional every day for a week. Journal about your different insights each day.

❑ Select a devotional book and ask a friend or mentor to read it with you. Discuss your experiences and discoveries.

Lectio Divina

Signs of the Spirit

Discuss where you have seen God's Spirit at work this week. How have you experienced grace in a new way through Christian practice? Discuss any joys or struggles you had. How is it with your soul?

Purpose

Because we long for Christ to be formed in us, we make this covenant to tend the fires of our souls so that our longing for Christ may never be extinguished and that our lives will be set ablaze with his love.

> When in reading Scripture you meet with a passage that seems to give your heart a new motion toward God, turn it into the form of a petition, and give it a place in your prayers.
> —William Law
> (1686-1761)

Instruction

Lectio divina. So what's that? Some kind of strange-sounding disease? The Latin term for an insect? No—it's something much better than that! *Lectio* means "reading" and *divina* means "spiritual" or "holy." *Spiritual reading*—the name itself is a clue that this way of reading is clearly different from the way we might read a textbook, a sports magazine, or a favorite website.

In this way of approaching the Bible, we are looking for something more than information. We are looking for formation. We are seeking to be transformed and renewed by God (see Romans 12:2) and to have the "mind of Christ" (see Philippians 2:5-8). Lectio divina is a reflective and prayerful kind of reading. It is about quality, not quantity. It is about going deeper, not about covering a lot of territory.

In a way, instead of our reading the Bible, we open ourselves and allow the Bible to "read" us. Have you ever experienced reading a verse in the Bible that seemed to be written just for you, that hit you right where you live? The power of God's Word is vividly described in Hebrews 4:12: "Indeed, the word of God is living and active, sharper than any two-edged sword, piercing until it divides soul from spirit, joints from marrow; it is able to judge the thoughts and intentions of the heart." Discuss: How do we open ourselves to hearing the powerful Word of God?

Allowing the Bible to Read Us

Lectio divina goes back a long way to the Jewish tradition of meditating on Scripture. You can see this practice in Psalm 1:1-2: "Happy are those who . . . delight . . . in the law of the LORD, and on his law they meditate day and night." In the sixth century, Saint Benedict refined this practice for monastic communities; and in the centuries since, both Roman Catholics and Protestants have widely used this form of reading the Bible.

With a partner, discuss your current style of reading the Bible. Do you have a consistent practice? What keeps you from delving in? What would it take to get you started?

Perhaps this way of reading Scripture is already familiar to you. When something in Scripture catches your attention, you stop reading and think about it some more. In the same way you chew your food, you process and reprocess this spiritual food until it is more fully digested by your heart and mind.

When you practice lectio divina, you will want to choose a short passage of Scripture, maybe four to eight verses. Read together the steps of lectio divina:

> The manner of spiritual reading is like drinking in the words of a love letter or pondering the meaning of a poem. It is not like skittering over the surface of a popular magazine or plowing through a computer manual. We are seeking not merely information but formation.
>
> —Marjorie Thompson, *Soul Feast* [1]

❖ First, invite God to speak to you through Scripture and prepare yourself to listen.

❖ Read the Scripture through once, then again, slowly. Read it aloud a few times. Listen for the word or phrase that attracts you or seems to stand out from the rest of the words.

❖ Reflect on what the words mean in the phrase that sticks with you. "Chew" on the words for awhile. What is God trying to say to you?

❖ Respond to God in prayer about what God has said to you in the Scripture. Are you thankful? sad? angry? guilty? enlightened? How does the Scripture move you to pray?

❖ Rest in God's presence and simply enjoy the nearness of God.

❖ Record your experience or any insight you receive during this time.

Have someone read aloud the quotation from Marjorie Thompson. Discuss the difference between the way you read a letter from your best friend, boyfriend, or girlfriend whom you haven't seen in awhile and then the way you would read a school textbook or instruction manual. What are you looking for in the letter? What are you looking for in the textbook? Which way do you generally read the Bible?

Read together the words from Teresa of Avila on page 52. Discuss the mystery of God's revelation to us in the Holy Word. How might practicing lectio divina draw us closer to the mystery?

 ## ehearsal

Try lectio divina as a group. Using Mark 4:35-41 and the instructions on the previous page, light a candle and say together, "This represents the light and presence of Christ in our midst right now."
Sing together "Thy Word" or another familiar song about God's Word and begin your time of spiritual reading. Allow three to five minutes of silence and close by saying, "Amen." Discuss any insights, struggles, comfort levels, and so forth after having practiced lectio divina. In the space below write down anything that God may have whispered to you in the Scripture passage.

> We should accept with simplicity whatever understanding the Lord gives us; and what he doesn't we shouldn't tire ourselves over. For one word of God's will contains within itself a thousand mysteries.
> —Teresa of Avila
> (1515-1582)

 ## nvolving

What kind of ripples might (or have) come about from practicing lectio divina? How could your daily routine change by the transformation taking place in your soul? Discuss how you might see all areas of your life—home, school, nature, community, world, job, paying bills, and so forth—connected in a new way based on your spiritual formation journey.

 ## omorrow

❑ Experience lectio divina online at *www.methodx.net/connect/lectio.asp*. You'll be led through the passage, step by step. You can even journal online.

❑ Read the same passage of Scripture for five days, using the steps of lectio divina. You might be surprised at the many ways that the same Scripture can speak to your life. Suggested texts: Psalm 63:1-8; Jeremiah 1:4-9; Micah 6:8; Habakkuk 3:17-19; Luke 24:28-32; or Colossians 3:1-3.

❑ Use a concordance to search for Scripture on an interesting topic or question. Read a different Scripture passage about that topic daily, using the lectio divina process. Write your insights in a journal.

Notes
1 Reprinted from *Soul Feast: An Invitation to the Christian Spiritual Life* by Marjorie J. Thompson. © 1995 by Marjorie J. Thompson. Used by permission.

Chastity

Signs of the Spirit

Discuss where you have seen God's Spirit at work this week. How have you experienced grace in a new way through Christian practice? Discuss any joys or struggles you had. How is it with your soul?

Purpose

Because we long for Christ to be formed in us, we make this covenant to tend the fires of our souls so that our longing for Christ may never be extinguished and that our lives will be set ablaze with his love.

Instruction

Chastity is not a common word in our culture, nor is it probably a very popular one. What comes to mind at the mention of the word? Monks locked away in their monasteries praying in sackcloth? a strict standard of purity and abstinence? In a culture where complex relationships are broken and mended in a thirty-minute sitcom and barely dressed men and women sell everything from underwear to cars, does chastity even seem realistic?

Chastity Isn't

A better understanding of chastity will help us as we struggle with the realities of friendships, romantic relationships, and physical intimacy and how they affect our life-formation. First, chastity is not synonymous with *celibacy*, which means to abstain from sexual relations or marriage. Rather, chastity means letting go of the "I want" and "I must have" mentality that often drives our emotional and physical relationships. Have you ever been in a relationship or observed a relationship in which one person is totally absorbed in it, consuming his or her thoughts, time, and energy? How has that one relationship affected the person's state of mind and other relationships? Talk about those relationships as a group.

Secondly, chastity is not a difficult burden forced upon us to keep us from enjoying love and intimacy. Instead it is an intentional effort to keep God at the center of all relationships. Chaste persons see God in one another, surrender self-centeredness in relationships, and do not attempt possession over the person or the relationship. Persons practicing chastity do not eliminate love, contain their desire for love, nor avoid physical intimacy, but they prayerfully seek to make God the

center of each relationship. In doing so, they make love the center. Chastity means viewing every relationship (romantic or platonic) and sex as God's good gifts and learning how best to receive, care for, and share those gifts with others.

In 1 Thessalonians 4:1–8, Paul talks about how we ought to respect and care for one another. Read the Scripture aloud and discuss what chastity means in light of Paul's teaching. To what did God call us in this passage?

Chastity Is

The virtue of chastity is a way of life, a call, to consider carefully and prayerfully how you will care for both your spirit and body and the spirit and body of anyone with whom you are in relationship. Different people practicing chastity may choose differing levels of emotional and physical intimacy in relationships. According to *The Catholic Encyclopedia*, the practice of chastity "springs from the dignity of human nature." When making decisions one must view all persons as children of God, worthy of the utmost respect and care.

❖ What changes might you see in romantic relationships and sexual activity if everyone first considered themselves and one another as children of God?

❖ Would this change in perspective affect the way you or your friends make decisions about relationships and sexual activity? How?

❖ Each of us must do the difficult work of examining our motives and actions in the light of our faith and spiritual formation journey. Because chastity means respecting ourselves and all others, the virtue does imply some boundaries. List below any limits that your parents set for you regarding dating relationships.

❖ Next list any guidelines for sexual activity that you have received from parents, teachers, pastors, or youth ministers.

❖ Finally, list any boundaries or limits that you have set for yourself.

Talk about what influences or sources have helped you to set your own boundaries and discuss the ways in which practicing chastity might affect how you present yourself.

❖ How might the way you conduct your relationships change?

In our culture pure and truly intimate relationships are not the dominant form of interaction. Most relationships are short-term and only skim the intimate surface. In romantic relationships, it is often hard to practice chastity. Hormones and peer pressure often get the best of us. Sex is a gift from God, and it is good; but it can also be abused and harmful to us when we do not make God the center of our relationships. Practicing chastity can give us balance and help us stay within our boundaries.

Read the story below about Alice. How is she practicing or not practicing the spiritual discipline of chastity?

Alice is a seventeen-year-old young woman who began dating at age fourteen. She started dating Tony when she was a freshman and he was a senior. They saw each other on Wednesday and Sunday nights at youth group and then would hang out with his friends after football games on Fridays. They usually studied together or went to a movie on Saturdays. They had much in common but broke up when he left for college. She didn't find out until after he left that her friends were hurt about how little time she had spent with them.

Alice met Dylan at church camp where they were both junior counselors. They knew they would only be together for a couple months before school started again, so they spent as much time as they could together. Often their late night talks ended with a lot of kissing and touching. Alice didn't know if what they were doing was OK, but by the time she started to think about their actions, camp was almost over anyway. She didn't want to bring it up and ruin a great summer.

Now Alice is interested in Gary, with whom she works after school at the pet store. They have gone out a couple times this month. They can't go out much more than that because Gary always goes out with his friends on Friday nights. But he said he would like to meet her friends, and she invited him to come to youth group. They talk a lot at work; and they have been honest about past relationships, doubts, and fears. Alice thinks she would be OK talking with him about how comfortable she is with physical intimacy, if they continue to date.

Can you think of other situations you have been in or friends you know of who have have had similar experiences to Alice's story? How could practicing chastity help us consistently have godly, healthy relationships?

 ehearsal

Read Song of Solomon, chapters 2 and 3.

❖ How do the bride and groom understand or describe their relationship and sexuality?

❖ How do their views differ from or reflect those you listed above?

❖ How is the Song of Solomon the same as or different than the love songs you hear on the radio today?

nvolving

What kind of ripples might (or have) come about from practicing chastity? How could your daily routine change by the transformation taking place in your soul? Discuss how you might see all areas of your life—home, school, nature, community, world, job, paying bills, and so forth—connected in a new way based on your spiritual formation journey.

omorrow

❑ Pray and journal about your romantic relationship. Do you have a steady boyfriend or girlfriend? Are you "dating around"? How might practicing chastity affect your relationship? In what ways could you have an honest discussion with your boyfriend or girlfriend about levels of intimacy, boundaries such as time spent together, activities you did together, places you went on dates, physical intimacy, and so forth? How can your relationship be pure and centered around God's love?

❑ Ask a trusted adult if he or she would discuss with you, openly and honestly, about intimate relationships and chastity. Ask the adult to talk about his or her boundaries and how they were established.

❑ Answer these questions in your journal: What word or words would you use to describe a dating relationship? to describe sex? What words would your parents choose? your best friend? your youth minister? your campus minister? How are these descriptions similar or unlike what we learn from Scripture?

❑ Evaluate your relationships to see if God is at the center of each of them. Pray several times daily for each relationship you are in. Pray that God would be the foundation upon which the relationship was built and that purity and dignity would be priorities.

Fasting

igns of the Spirit

Discuss where you have seen God's Spirit at work this week. How have you experienced grace in a new way through Christian practice? Discuss any joys or struggles you had. How is it with your soul?

urpose

Because we long for Christ to be formed in us, we make this covenant to tend the fires of our souls so that our longing for Christ may never be extinguished and that our lives will be set ablaze with his love.

nstruction

What Is Fasting?

Fasting, abstaining from food accompanied by prayer and meditation, is a regular part of the Hebrew story as witnessed in the biblical text. In the Old Testament, the Jewish Queen Esther commands all Jews to observe a three-day fast in preparation for her plan to save the people. In the Acts of the Apostles, Paul, who is a devout Jew prior to his conversion, reacts instinctively with fasting and prayer to his blinding experience with the risen Christ on the road to Damascus.

As the Christian church grew, the regular practice of fasting continued among the early Christians. An anonymous document known as the *Didache*, or *The Teachings of the Apostles*, from the first or second century, directs followers of Jesus to continue the regular practice of fasting on Wednesdays and Fridays, unlike the Jewish observance of the fast on Mondays and Thursdays.

Editor's note: The object of fasting as we speak of it here is not to lose or control one's weight or to punish ourselves. The rigorous and strict abstention from food for extended periods of time as a form of weight loss, diet control, or penance can be both psychologically and physically damaging to our bodies. If you are dealing with issues of self-image that lead you to any type of eating disorder, please seek the help of a parent, counselor, minister, or physician.

John Wesley, the founder of Methodism, followed the tradition of the early church and continued the spiritual practice of fasting on Wednesdays and Fridays throughout most of his adult life. Wesley believed that one can observe the fast in three ways: abstaining from food, abstaining from particular foods (such as meat), or abstaining from rich or pleasant foods (such as decadent dishes or desserts). Wesley believed that the fast is an instituted or required means of grace but one that has the potential to be abused by those seeking something other than a deeper relationship with God.

Why Do We Fast?

Fasting is the abstention completely from one's normal daily intake of food. Fasting as a Christian practice does not restrict the fast to food. Fasting can also be the abstention from things that occupy time that would be better spent focused on our relationship with Christ, such as watching television, surfing the Net, or engaging in the latest gossip. Sorry, abstaining from homework is not an option (nice try).

Abstention in this form may be a much safer option if you are, because of medical reasons, unable to abstain from food. The object of the fast is to free time and energy normally spent focusing on our worldly needs to focus our time and energy on our spiritual needs through practices like prayer, meditation and contemplation, or reading the Bible.

Fasting should never be practiced for weight loss. Your health should never be compromised while fasting. If you have problems with your self-image or are struggling with an eating disorder, it would be better for you to fast from something else in your life, such as television, talking on the phone, a bad habit, and so forth.

❖ What would you choose to abstain from for a fast?

❖ How would you use the time and energy to focus on God?'

> And whenever you fast, do not look dismal, like the hypocrites, for they disfigure their faces so as to show others that they are fasting. Truly I tell you, they have received their reward. But when you fast, put oil on your head and wash your face, so that your fasting may be seen not by others but by your Father who is in secret; and your Father who sees in secret will reward you.
> —Matthew 6:16-18

Observing the fast helps us to focus in times of struggle or decision, as well as times of deep spiritual or biblical study. When I am faced with a big decision or dealing with a particular issue concerning my faith, I find observing a fast helpful to focus my time and energy on prayer and meditation. A pastor I know, who has a tough time observing the fast, was inspired to persevere when the youth he led in a small group Bible study all decided to fast with him. They did this in an attempt to enrich their Bible study and devote themselves to prayer before each meeting. They would begin their fast after dinner the night before their meetings and break their fast by going out to a local restaurant and eating a meal together following the Bible study.

How Do We Fast?

In the passage from Matthew, Jesus provides us with clear instructions as to how we should observe our fast. Our fast is practiced before and for God and never for the attention or regard of others. This directive does not mean that you must keep your fast completely secret. Letting those people close to you (like a parent or guardian) know about your fast spares them the potential worry or embarrassment of inadvertent temptation and offers them the chance to support your endeavors through prayer.

Jesus also says to those gathered in his presence to "put oil upon your head and wash your face." His command means that as you observe the fast, you should go about your daily routine of cleaning and preparing yourself for the world around you. Don't look dismal as a way to publicize your fast. Let the fast be a time of joy for you as you take the opportunity to spend time with God.

❖ Why should those who are fasting not draw attention to their action?

How Long Should I Fast?

Set realistic goals for yourself as you observe the fast and start slowly by abstaining from one meal or one daily habit. John Wesley observed the fast from sundown the day before until dusk on the day of his fast; for him, this constituted an entire day. The goal of going one day a week without food or a part of our daily routine is a realistic one for some. For others, fasting may be a less frequent practice.

Remember that if you abstain from food during your fast, you should drink plenty of fluids like water or juice. Side effects you may experience during a fast from food include a growling stomach, hunger pains, headaches, and bad breath. Also be aware that as you observe your fast, you should not engage in any form of strenuous activity or exercise. If you are involved in any type of sport or extracurricular activity that requires this type of activity, observe your fast on days you do not practice or play. Choose days that help you stick with your commitment.

 ehearsal

Discuss any questions or fears you have about fasting.

Consider persons in our world who are genuinely hungry because of the lack of resources. How can fasting help us understand or meet the needs of the malnourished? Make a plan to observe a group fast to help meet the needs of others, such as giving money you would normally spend on fast food in a month to hunger relief. You may choose instead to meet at a time you would normally devote to dinner or lunch and serve a meal at a local food bank or soup kitchen.

One way to break a fast is by taking Communion. Before the next meeting, agree when you could observe the fast by either abstaining from food or a daily activity. Break your fast by inviting your pastor to serve Communion. Or break your fast over a group meal at a local restaurant or potluck dinner following your next group meeting.

nvolving

What kind of ripples might (or have) come about from practicing fasting? How could your daily routine change by the transformation taking place in your soul? Discuss how you might see all areas of your life—home, school, nature, community, world, job, paying bills, and so forth—connected in a new way based on your spiritual formation journey.

omorrow

❑ Journalist Catherine Marshall writes about God's calling her to fast from her habit of criticism. Fast from at least one bad habit for a week and journal about it, using these questions:
  ❖ What was it that challenged you most in fasting from this bad habit?
  ❖ Did you find anything positive to replace this habit and help keep your focus?
  ❖ Was prayer involved in your fast? If so, for what did you pray?
  ❖ Will you go back to practicing this habit, or did your fast help you overcome it?

❑ Use a concordance to search Scripture for the word *fasting*. While reading each passage, answer these questions:
  ❖ When and why do the people in these passages observe the fast?
  ❖ What is the result of their observance of the fast?
  ❖ What do these passages have to say about my experience with fasting?

❑ Visit *www.30hourfamine.org* to get information about hosting the 30 Hour Famine. In this fundraiser for World Vision, you raise money by soliciting donations from people for every hour you agree to observe the famine (fast). During this event you abstain from food and focus on games, service activities, and devotionals. You break the fast with a group meal.

Soul-Tending: Life-Forming Practices for Older Youth & Young Adults

Keeping the Sabbath

Signs of the Spirit

Discuss where you have seen God's Spirit at work this week. How have you experienced grace in a new way through Christian practice? Discuss any joys or struggles you had. How is it with your soul?

Purpose

Because we long for Christ to be formed in us, we make this covenant to tend the fires of our souls so that our longing for Christ may never be extinguished and that our lives will be set ablaze with his love.

Instruction

❖ Before you begin, take some time and write down your first impressions of the word *Sabbath*.

> The Israelite people shall keep the sabbath, observing the sabbath throughout the ages as a covenant for all time: it shall be a sign for all time between Me and the people of Israel. For in six days the LORD made heaven and earth, on the seventh day He ceased from work and was refreshed.
> —Exodus 31:16-17
> (TANAKH)

❖ What images come to mind when you think of the word *Sabbath*?

❖ What does it mean to keep the Sabbath? Why is it important to you?

The Meaning of Sabbath

The word *Sabbath* is derived from the Hebrew word *shavat*, meaning "to cease and desist." This definition gives us some indication of what Sabbath is all about. Sabbath is referred to a number of times in the Old Testament. In Exodus 20:1-17 and Deuteronomy 5:1-21, the observance of Sabbath on the seventh day of the week as a holy day is commanded. The passage from Exodus is part of a dialogue between God and Moses at Mount Sinai. In this dialogue, God lays down the purpose of the Sabbath as both a covenant between God and the people of Israel and a day of rest to be observed faithfully.

❖ Do you observe a time of ceasing and desisting from daily busyness?

Keeping the Sabbath Throughout Our History as God's People

As the Jewish faith developed, rituals for keeping the Sabbath also developed and evolved. Today, practicing Jewish persons observe Sabbath from sundown Friday until sundown Saturday. According to the Jewish calendar, Saturday is the seventh day of the week.

In contrast, the early Christian church observed Sabbath on Sunday to recognize Christ's resurrection and the work of the Holy Spirit on the first day of the week. In the Gospels, Jesus and some of the Pharisees (those who believe in the strict observance of the Law both inside and outside of the Temple) clash over how they understand the Sabbath. Jesus taught that the Sabbath was created for people to worship the Lord, not to discourage one from doing the work of the Lord. Keeping the Sabbath for Jesus was doing the work of the Lord, which for him was healing the sick and caring for the poor in spirit. The Pharisees did not agree. They understood that one keeps the Sabbath by ceasing totally from all physical labor, including what Jesus calls the work of the Lord.

As the Christian church developed, so did Christian education and corporate worship, which is how we continue to keep the Sabbath today. We, as the Christian church, keep the Sabbath by ceasing or sacrificing our regular schedule and resting from the busyness of our lives. We attend Sunday school and worship where we embrace and feast upon God's presence in our lives.

Four Ways to Keep the Sabbath

Ceasing: work, stress

Resting: spiritually, physically, emotionally, and intellectually

Embracing: Christian values, time, giving, wholeness, the world

Feasting: on the Eternal with music, beauty, food, and affection

—Adapted from *Keeping the Sabbath Wholly* by Marva J. Dawn

Sacrificing on the Sabbath

Ask someone to read aloud Numbers 28:9-10. These verses explain that an extra or doubling of offerings is required for the people of Israel to keep the Sabbath. Think about what, if anything, you sacrifice on the Sabbath and list your responses in the space below.

Keeping Time Holy on the Sabbath

The idea that the Sabbath is not just for Sunday is not a new one. Sabbath can be observed at any time of the week you choose. As it is with other disciplines such as fasting, Sabbath is not just about what we don't do but about what we choose to do with our time. In ceasing from the schedule of our everyday lives, we free up time to truly rest, to embrace wholly our relationship with God, and to feast on God's presence in our lives. There is a sense, then, that we can somehow regain that time we spend on unfocused busyness to sanctify it and make it holy. Rabbi Abraham Joshua Heschel, in his book *The Sabbath*, shares this idea about regaining our time and making it holy when he calls the Sabbath, "a palace in time which we build." Take some time to think about how you make your time holy on the Sabbath. Write your thoughts in the space below.

Holy Play on the Sabbath

The Sabbath is God's gift to us so that we will always have a day to rest, play, and enjoy God's amazing creation. Resting on the Sabbath does not mean sitting on the couch for twenty-four hours. Do you remember the last time you set aside a day for absolutely nothing? Do you have any hobbies or interests that you simply don't have time for? How might you experience God's rest while you spend time on your hobby? List below any hobbies you have been neglecting or have a desire to start. Talk to one another about those hobbies.

 ehearsal

Take some time to reflect on how you keep the Sabbath and answer these questions:

❖ What do you cease on the Sabbath?

❖ How do you rest on the Sabbath?

❖ What do you embrace on the Sabbath?

❖ How do you feast on the Sabbath?

Marva J. Dawn suggests that the main benefit of keeping Sabbath is that we cease trying to be God in our lives and let God care for us. List the benefits you now receive from keeping the Sabbath. What might be holding you back from enjoying the full benefits of holy rest and play?

nvolving

What kind of ripples might (or have) come about from practicing keeping the Sabbath? How could your daily routine change by the transformation taking place in your soul? Discuss how you might see all areas of your life—home, school, nature, community, world, job, paying bills, and so forth—connected in a new way based on your spiritual formation journey.

omorrow

❏ Before going to bed this Saturday night, read Exodus 31:13-17 and reflect on the busyness and work of your week. Make a list of ways you will cease from your work and truly rest on Sunday. Pray that God will give you the strength and ability to rest. On Sunday night write down your thoughts on what, if any, difference your Saturday night preparation made in helping you keep the Sabbath.

❏ Observe a time of Sabbath during the week if Sunday is too busy with church activities. On your chosen day of Sabbath, spend time doing the thing you love and thank God for the gift of Sabbath.

❏ Schedule a Sabbath retreat for your group. Invite a mentor to come and lead you in devotions and prayer. Spend an entire weekend basking in the love of God.

Forgiveness

Signs of the Spirit

Discuss where you have seen God's Spirit at work this week. How have you experienced grace in a new way through Christian practice? Discuss any joys or struggles you had. How is it with your soul?

Purpose

Because we long for Christ to be formed in us, we make this covenant to tend the fires of our souls so that our longing for Christ may never be extinguished and that our lives will be set ablaze with his love.

> For you, O LORD, are good and forgiving, abounding in steadfast love to all who call on you.
>
> —Psalm 86:5

Instruction

People are not perfect. You can't always count on others to treat you fairly. And believe it or not, they are not depending on you to always have their best interests at heart either. Since you crawled out of bed this morning, how many people have crossed your path? How many of those have done something to disappoint you or hurt your feelings? How many of those have been damaged by your quick-tongue or knee-jerk reactions?

We might not even be conscious of how we hurt others. We might just let the jabs that come our way roll right off our backs. Forgiveness for the little scrapes and scratches in our day-to-day relationships might just happen. But sometimes we can be wounded clear to the core of our being. Sometimes our words and actions draw blood and cut others deeply. Then there are awful tragedies, real crimes, and horrible injustices, when forgiveness becomes an issue of faith!

God Loves to Forgive

Forgiveness is at the heart of God. God yearns to forgive, aches to forgive, and hurries to forgive. Forgiveness proves that the power of love is stronger than anything that might separate us from God. Turn to the person next to you and talk about how you have experienced God's forgiveness.

Me? Forgive Others?

What if you were bullied, held by police for no reason, or raped? What if a friend were killed by a drunk driver? What would your gut-level reaction be? Anger? revenge? retaliation? or forgiveness? Be honest and talk to one another out of your own experience. What does it mean to forgive? How have your attempts at forgiveness been received? Write any thoughts or insights below.

Me? Forgive Me?

Sometimes we can't stand to face the one who stares back at us from the mirror. Sometimes God's forgiveness doesn't seem to cut through. Even efforts by others to help us forgive ourselves are blocked. Write about a time of unspeakable hurt, loss, or disappointment in your life. Why is forgiving yourself so hard? What barriers keep you from loving yourself as God loves you?

> And forgive us our debts, as we also have forgiven our debtors. For if you … forgive others their trespasses, your heavenly Father will also forgive you; but if you do not forgive others, neither will your Father forgive your trespasses.
> —Matthew 6:12, 14-15

What does forgiveness have to do with your spiritual life and relationship with God? What difference does God's forgiveness make in your life? What does forgiving others have to do with your faith? When we are forgiven, our gut-level anger and knee-jerk desire to get even die. A new attitude of the heart—a new impulse to forgive—comes to life in us as we realize God's forgiveness in our hearts.

What would the world be like if we really accepted the power of forgiveness to change hearts and give new life?

Jesus teaches that we are forgiven even as we forgive. Forgiveness is in our best interest! It's part of the faithful life of a believer. Peter was trying hard to get it right when he asked Jesus, "How often should I forgive?" (Matthew 18:21). For Jesus it's not how much you forgive; it's acting on the impulse to forgive. Take a minute to discuss this section.

 ehearsal

Think of a situation that could use some forgiveness. The event can either be from your own life or one you create. Anonymously write your own "Dear Abby" letter to describe what's happening. Ask someone to collect all the letters and shuffle them. Read a few of the letters, one at a time, as you rehearse the spiritual practice of forgiveness. Put your heads together and give advice that might lead a letter writer down the path of forgiveness.

Apply Matthew 6:12 to the situation described in a letter. What are the debts (on both sides) that need to be canceled out and forgiven?

Often when we struggle with forgiveness, we look for "loop holes" to excuse our need to forgive, such as:

❖ comparing ("It's not as bad as what she or he did.")
❖ minimizing ("It's not so bad, really.")
❖ defending ("He had it coming.")
❖ justifying ("I really had no choice. She or he deserved it.")

❖ Talk about your experiences with getting beyond these excuses.

 nvolving

What kind of ripples might (or have) come about from practicing forgiveness? How could your daily routine change by the transformation taking place in your soul? Discuss how you might see all areas of your life—home, school, nature, community, world, job, paying bills, and so forth—connected in a new way based on your spiritual formation journey.

 omorrow

❑ Commit to surrounding yourself with friends who consistently seek to offer and receive forgiveness. Be a witnesses of God's forgiveness for one another and for the world.

❑ Before you go to sleep each night this week, take a brief inventory of your day. From whom do you need to seek forgiveness? Pray for God's forgiveness and commit to seeking forgiveness immediately.

❑ Three times this week, read about Jesus and forgiveness in Matthew 9:2-8; Matthew 18:21-35; and Luke 7:36-50. How does Jesus encourage forgiveness? What is Jesus saying to you about forgiveness? Journal about how you could be a more forgiving person.

Bible Study

 ## igns of the Spirit

Discuss where you have seen God's Spirit at work this week. How have you experienced grace in a new way through Christian practice? Discuss any joys or struggles you had. How is it with your soul?

 ## urpose

Because we long for Christ to be formed in us, we make this covenant to tend the fires of our souls so that our longing for Christ may never be extinguished and that our lives will be set ablaze with his love.

 ## nstruction

Did you know that in Greek there are five different words with similar but distinct meanings that are all translated "love" in the English language? Or that there are two different accounts of creation in the book of Genesis? Have you noticed that in the Gospel of Matthew the phrase, "this occurred in order to fulfill what was spoken by the prophet" is mentioned several times throughout the Gospel? Are these just interesting facts to impress your friends, or do they tell us important things about our history, tradition, and who God is?

A Story of Us

The Bible tells the story from beginning to end of God's making the world in love, the world's rejection of God, and God's continual effort to be in relationship with creation. The Bible is the story of us. It contains our past, present, and future. It is not just history and poetry and stories, but a message from God. Through Bible study, God reveals truth and wisdom to us.

❖ Do you look to the Bible to help answer questions you encounter in your personal life or in the world around you? List below some of those concerns and issues.

Soul-Tending: Life-Forming Practices for Older Youth & Young Adults

Do you know where to begin to search the Bible for the answers you seek? If so, how does the Bible help you answer or help you deal with the concerns you listed? If not, to whom can you turn for help in understanding the Bible?

A Controversial Book

In every denomination, church, and even family, disputes go on about how to read and understand the Bible. Is the Bible the only source for wisdom? Is every word of the Bible inspired, or God-breathed and without error? Is the Bible consistent on every issue throughout the Old and New Testaments? Is the Bible historically accurate? As you grow in your faith and encounter these questions, you will find it helpful to know where to look for information that will allow us to make decisions. It is important that each of us seeks answers to these questions.

> ❖ Discuss this statement: The Bible can be used to defend and refute the same issues.

At any price, give me the book of God! Here is knowledge enough for me. In God's presence I open, I read this book, for this end: to find the way to heaven.
—John Wesley

Knowledge and Discipleship

Someone read aloud 2 Peter 1:3–8. The second letter of Peter teaches that knowledge is essential to discipleship. Stanley Hauerwas, a professor of ethics, insists that "discipleship is required for the right reading of Scripture." The faith journey is a cycle of study, reflection, and action that helps us to be faithful disciples of Jesus Christ. Discuss how you see Bible study and discipleship working together to help you grow in faith.

Just as you are students of history, algebra, chemistry, and English, you are also theologians, persons who study God. Bible study can be an exciting part of your faith journey as you begin to understand the roots of many traditions, make sense of your spiritual experiences, and practice your reasoning skills to wrestle with the hard things of life.

 ehearsal

Many tools are available to assist you in your study and understanding of the Bible. Ask your youth minister or pastor to provide you with Bible dictionaries, concordances, and different commentaries on the Bible. Divide into three groups to study and discuss the following:

❖ Group 1: Look up the words *faith*, *hope*, and *love* in the Bible dictionary. What new information do you find there? What is interesting? What is surprising?

❖ Group 2: Look up the word *youth* in a concordance. How many references are there to youth in the Bible? Are they mostly in the Old or New Testaments? Do these references apply to your life today? How?

❖ Group 3: Read Genesis 1:1-2:4a and Genesis 2:4b-3. Then read one or more commentaries on those chapters. What did you learn? With what do you agree or disagree?

Discuss what was new and interesting in this discovery. Does it help you understand God in a new way? How could Bible study strengthen you as a disciple of Christ?

nvolving

What kind of ripples might (or have) come about from practicing Bible study? How could your daily routine change by the transformation taking place in your soul? Discuss how you might see all areas of your life—home, school, nature, community, world, job, paying bills, and so forth—connected in a new way based on your spiritual formation journey.

omorrow

❑ Using the tools discussed, spend some time this week finding more information on a topic about which you have questions.

❑ Check your Bible or go to your pastor's office, church library, or local library and look for maps during Jesus' lifetime. Find Bethlehem, Judea, and Nazareth. Get to know the land that Jesus walked.

❑ Skim a Bible concordance. What topics included there surprised you? Which topics seem to be missing? Choose a topic to research and spend time studying.

❑ Find a study Bible with footnotes. Read Proverbs 2:1-15. Then read the footnotes. Do the footnotes provide interesting and helpful information? Read the passage again. What do you understand better or differently now?

❑ Read your favorite Bible passage in several different Bible translations, such as the New International Version, New Revised Standard Version, and the Contemporary English Versions. What differences and similarities do you notice? Are the different translations helpful or confusing? What new insights do you gain from reading the different versions?

Self-denial

 igns of the Spirit

Discuss where you have seen God's Spirit at work this week. How have you experienced grace in a new way through Christian practice? Discuss any joys or struggles you had. How is it with your soul?

 urpose

Because we long for Christ to be formed in us, we make this covenant to tend the fires of our souls so that our longing for Christ may never be extinguished and that our lives will be set ablaze with his love.

> If any want to become my followers, let them deny themselves and take up their cross and follow me.
> —Mark 8:34

 nstruction

Athletes do it. Musicians do it. Artists do it. Our parents even do it for our benefit. We see forms of self-denial all around us. Yet self-denial is among the most difficult of Jesus' teachings. It is basically this: When we deny ourselves, we give up something or choose one path instead of another. Self-denial is a reminder that following Jesus is a way of life, not a one-time decision. One of the earliest Christian teachings, *The Didache*, begins with, "There are two ways: one of Life—one of Death. There are great differences between these two ways" (*The Didache*, 1.1).

Choosing Christ Above Ourselves

In his epistles, the apostle Paul repeatedly spoke of changing our lives and of denying ourselves for Christ. The early Christians faced daily persecution and challenges, often struggling to maintain a Christian life. John Wesley preached and studied heavily the subject of self-denial in an attempt to encourage his congregations to grow spiritually. Although the world was different in both of these men's times, today's Christians face many of the same issues, and this practice is still essential to our lives as Christians—followers of Christ.

"If we do not continually deny ourselves, we do not learn of Him ... If we do not take up our cross daily, we do not come after Him, but after the world, we are not walking in the way of the cross, we are not following Him" (John Wesley, Sermon 48).

It's Not Easy!

Self-denial is a difficult practice for several reasons. First, discerning what is the right decision is not always easy. Sometimes a choice may appear appealing, yet it can be destructive. As Christians we have the ability to choose wisely even when the choice is difficult. Romans 2:15 tells us that God's law is not foreign to us, but it is woven into the fabric of our very creation. Something deep within us echoes God's yes and no and tells us right and wrong.

Second, we cannot do everything. At times we take on too much, and we pay the price. Thinking we can do it all can be the sin of pride. In one way or another we suffer and others may, too, as a result. Sometimes we can't keep our commitments, we blow up at someone, or we burnout.

Third, we can have a hard time focusing to select the one activity that is the best for us. The messages sent to us by the media lead us to desires that compete for our attention. When we simplify our lives, we discover the best thing for us. Think about Jesus' teaching to Mary and Martha in Luke 10.

Fourth, self-denial can be difficult when the choice is very clear, and we recognize that God is calling us to do something that is not pleasurable or enjoyable. Think of this as what it means to take up the cross—to intentionally serve others in a sacrificial way.

> They show that what the law requires is written on their hearts, to which their own conscience also bears witness.
>
> —Romans 2:15

❖ Is there some area in your own life where you practice self-denial?

But There Is Joy

When we became Christians, each of us said: "Not myself, but Christ." We confirm this choice every day. The more we do this, the more joyful we will be. Great things happen when we deny ourselves and focus on what God calls us to do.

Jesus practiced self-denial. He was tempted to do many things (Matthew 4 or Luke 4), yet these many things were not God's purpose for his life. In his life we see the model for self-denial.

❖ To what temptations did Jesus say no?

❖ To what do you need to say no in your own life?

Ultimately Jesus denied his own will as he said, "Not what I want, but what you want" (Mark 14:36). Jesus taught us exactly what self-denial is in his willingness to lay down his life on our behalf. What can we learn about self-denial from Jesus' words in the garden? Write any thoughts below.

Rehearsal

Discuss how Jesus practiced self-denial. Think about his life, and record two or three biblical passages that give examples of this practice.

❖ What does it mean to pray, "not what I want, but what you want"?

❖ How, by resisting temptation, could you deny yourself and take up your cross?

Involving

What kind of ripples might (or have) come about from practicing self-denial? How could your daily routine change by the transformation taking place in your soul? Discuss how you might see all areas of your life—home, school, nature, community, world, job, paying bills, and so forth—connected in a new way based on your spiritual formation journey.

Tomorrow

❑ Spend time each day this week in prayer surrendering yourself to the will of God. Keep a journal and list the ways God has used you as a result of offering yourself so completely to God.

❑ Commit to giving something up this week that would benefit someone else. Give up your telephone time to go to the grocery store for your family; resist the temptation to gossip and instead say nice things about everyone with whom you come in contact; or volunteer at a nursing home, a food pantry, or a shelter instead of going out on the weekend.

❑ As you wake each day this week, pray the words of Jesus, "not what I want, but what you want" as a daily act of submitting to God's will.

Giving Thanks and Praise

 igns of the Spirit

Discuss where you have seen God's Spirit at work this week. How have you experienced grace in a new way through Christian practice? Discuss any joys or struggles you had. How is it with your soul?

 urpose

Because we long for Christ to be formed in us, we make this covenant to tend the fires of our souls so that our longing for Christ may never be extinguished and that our lives will be set ablaze with his love.

> Enter his gates with thanksgiving, and his courts with praise. Give thanks to him, bless his name.
> —Psalm 100:4

 nstruction

What prompts you to praise God? Is it a natural wonder, a special person, an accomplishment, a piece of music, a work of art, a faithful testimony, or a problem solved? How do you praise God? with dance? with trumpet and cymbals? with your mouth?

Looking to God

We can't praise if we don't look to God. We can't praise if we don't recognize God's hand in our lives. We can't praise until we accept and receive God's love. Discuss the following questions with a partner:

❖ When have you noticed God's help in your life?

❖ When have you caught a glimpse of God's strength?

❖ When have you heard God's voice speaking in your ear?

❖ How do you seek God?

❖ What helps you pay attention to God?

❖ How have you said yes to God's love?

Adoring God

Once our eyes are open to God's awesome love and power in our lives, we give thanks and turn our gaze toward God. We love and adore God. We cherish God's steadfast love in Christ. We treasure God's ever-present Spirit. We praise and bless God. In your mind's eye, sit and gaze at God. How do you express your adoration? your gratitude? your love? Write down what you hear yourself saying to God.

❖ What do expressions of thanksgiving and praise have to do with your spiritual life or your relationship with God?

❖ How might giving thanks and praise deepen your faith?

Recognizing God's majesty and greatness and expressing delight is a spiritual practice. We can fix the attitude of our souls to be in adoration and praise. It is good to celebrate God's nearness and love.

> Great is the LORD,
> and greatly to be
> praised.
> —Psalm 145:3a

A Matter of Focus

Thanksgiving is all about what God has done for us. Gratitude means taking nothing for granted. If faith is our response to God's presence in our lives, then expressions of thanks are at the heart of our spiritual lives. Take a look at Luke's account of the leper's healing in Luke 17:11-19. The man with leprosy recognized his healing as a sign of God's love. He said, "Thanks!" and his relationship with God rose to a new level. He wasn't just healed—he was saved!

Turn to someone and together make a list of what God has done for you. Be specific; you may list gifts such as a friendship, a second chance, or an act of mercy. How will you give thanks to God for all the blessings?

Praise focuses on the greatness of God. Read Psalm 145. What does this writer say about God? How many times does the writer say "praise"? Praise doesn't analyze, demand special favors, or greedily ask God to "do it again." Praise declares God's faithfulness, love, and compassion. Praise honors God for who God is. Praise claims utter dependence upon God's grace, mercy, and awesome love. Talk about what it means to praise God with delight.

 ehearsal

As a group, try the spiritual practice of giving thanks and praise. Praise God with delight! Read Psalm 150 as loud as possible together. Sing praise choruses.

 nvolving

What kind of ripples might (or have) come about from practicing giving thanks and praise? How could your daily routine change by the transformation taking place in your soul? Discuss how you might see all areas of your life—home, school, nature, community, world, job, paying bills, and so forth—connected in a new way based on your spiritual formation journey.

> Let us continually offer a sacrifice of praise to God, that is, the fruit of lips that confess his name.
> —Hebrews 13:15

 omorrow

❑ Explore the Scriptures. Look for a phrase, verse, or passage that moves you to give thanks and praise. Memorize it. Use this Scripture to center yourself for your daily prayers. First, give thanks for what God has done, then focus your thoughts on God and give praise.

❑ Set aside a time of fasting to help turn your gaze toward God. Spend your fast celebrating God's mighty acts by praising and giving thanks. This might be an especially meaningful time of preparation for the celebration of Holy Communion or the seasons of Advent and Lent.

❑ The Old Testament priests offered a sacrifice to God in the morning and in the evening. The writer of Hebrews offers this practice as a good starting place for believers. Begin each day by offering praises from your lips. End each day with prayers of thanksgiving.

❑ Adopt a "fussy" plant that is utterly dependent on your nurturing care. Let your tending time be a cue for you to give thanks and praise for all that God is to you.

Prayer From a Repentant Heart

igns of the Spirit

Discuss where you have seen God's Spirit at work this week. How have you experienced grace in a new way through Christian practice? Discuss any joys or struggles you had. How is it with your soul?

urpose

Because we long for Christ to be formed in us, we make this covenant to tend the fires of our souls so that our longing for Christ may never be extinguished and that our lives will be set ablaze with his love.

> Search me, O God, and know my heart; test me and know my anxious thoughts. See if there is any wicked way in me, and lead me in the way everlasting.
> —Psalm 139:23-24

nstruction

I can still hear the voice from a preacher at a youth camp I attended, "Repent today in case you die tonight!" The message from this well-meaning preacher was that unless we repented of our sins right at that moment, we would not be granted eternal life with God, nor merit God's love. I later learned that God's love for me did not depend on my sudden actions nor my fear of going to hell, but on my humble heart accepting and receiving God's love.

Not From Fear but From Love

God does not call us to repent because we are afraid of our eternal future. We are called to repent out of our love for God and our desire to have an intimate relationship with God through Jesus Christ. Discuss the following questions:

❖ In what situations have you heard the word *repent*?

❖ Have you ever been asked to repent of your sin?

❖ What do you think it means to repent?

To repent means to turn and go in the completely opposite direction. When John the Baptist calls out, "Repent, for the kingdom of heaven has come near" (Matthew 3:2), he is calling people to turn from their sin and begin a new life. In the same way, we are called to repent today. Jesus calls us to turn from our sin and begin our lives again in him. Discuss what it would mean to turn and go the opposite direction from sin. Write any thoughts or insights below.

Psalm 139 tells us just how well God knows us. God knows our insides and outsides, our comings and goings, our ups and downs, our thoughts near and far. God's intimate knowledge of us helps us understand repentance. Because we are so well known, we ought not be afraid to come to God with a repentant heart. Read together the entire psalm and discuss the following questions:

❖ What does it mean to you to be so completely known by God?

❖ How does this make you feel about coming to God in repentance?

❖ Why do you think the writer chose to end the psalm with a prayer of repentance?

❖ How would praying from a repentant heart nurture your faith and tend the needs of your soul?

How to Turn

Although the message is not explicit in the text, the writer of the psalm teaches us how to repent and how to live a life of faith. Break apart verses 23-24 and discuss how you might learn to repent and live faithfully:

❖ "Search me, O God, and know my heart."

❖ "Test me and know my thoughts."

❖ "See if there is any wicked way in me, and lead me in the way everlasting."

These verses teach us how to pray, asking God to search every part of our lives and take away all the sin that would separate us. When we have sin in our lives, we are not as close as God longs for us to be. Praying from a repentant heart means that God wipes away the sin and leads us in a completely new direction—the opposite direction from sin. When we are freed from our sin, we walk side-by-side with Jesus on our journey of faith. This closeness keeps us always attuned to his will for our lives.

ehearsal

Pray Psalm 139 again together very slowly and pause after each section or thought. Meditate on each phrase and ask God to examine each area of your life and remove the sin that separates the two of you. After your prayer, discuss how you feel. Do you feel released of your sin and confident in your faith walk? Do you feel intimidated by how well God knows you?

nvolving

What kind of ripples might (or have) come about from practicing prayer from a repentant heart? How could your daily routine change by the transformation taking place in your soul? Discuss how you might see all areas of your life—home, school, nature, community, world, job, paying bills, and so forth—connected in a new way based on your spiritual formation journey.

omorrow

❏ Memorize Psalm 139:23-24 and make it the beginning of your daily prayers. Journal about the new sense of closeness you feel to God.

❏ Study the places where the words *repent* or *repentance* appear in the Bible. Gain a full understanding of what Jesus means when he calls us to repent.

❏ Commit to praying for God to examine and clean out your heart each time you pray. Sin sneaks in and clutters our lives, so it is good to be in constant prayer against it.

Dying Well

 ## Signs of the Spirit

Discuss where you have seen God's Spirit at work this week. How have you experienced grace in a new way through Christian practice? Discuss any joys or struggles you had. How is it with your soul?

 ## Purpose

Because we long for Christ to be formed in us, we make this covenant to tend the fires of our souls so that our longing for Christ may never be extinguished and that our lives will be set ablaze with his love.

> Death—the last sleep? No, it is the final awakening.
> —Walter Scott

 ## Instruction

Just as surely as we came into this world at birth, our bodies will leave this world through death. Yet even though some would remind us that every day we live brings us closer to death, we focus on living, not on dying. Old people or sick people die, but the young are supposed to live for a long time. So why talk about dying when it seems years away?

First of all, as Christians, we know that death is not to be feared, so looking at death reminds us that "neither death, nor life, nor angels, nor rulers, nor things present, nor things to come, nor powers, nor heights, nor depth, nor anything else in all creation, will be able to separate us from the love of God in Christ Jesus our Lord" (Romans 8:38).

Second, all of us lose loved ones to death even if we remain healthy. How might we support family or friends who have cancer or other life-threatening diseases? How do we prepare ourselves for accidents that leave us bereft of a loved one? Finally and most importantly, exploring our feelings about death may also affect how we live our lives now.

I Don't Even Want to Go There. . .

In two minutes, list in the margins as many endings as possible to this sentence starter: Death is _____.

Now discuss all your possible sentence endings. Are there any recurring themes? What words would you use to describe people's feelings about death? Would you change anything on your list after hearing what others had to say?

What's Next?
Even though numerous studies claim people in near-death situations experience a great feeling of peace or see a bright light beckoning them, death still remains a great unknown. In pairs, discuss what you think happens after a person dies. What does the Bible say about life after death? Read the following verses, then discuss with your partner what they tell us about eternal life: John 3:16, John 6:40, John 14:1-5a, and Romans 6:22-23. Is it hard to trust God's promises?

Not Much Time Left
If you found out that you had only a short time left to live, how would you spend that time? Does the possibility of dying change how you think about living? What is the connection between life and death?

Your Obituary
We all hope that whenever we do die, we will be remembered for who we are, how we affected others' lives, and maybe even for an achievement or two. In the space below, write a brief obituary for yourself. For what would you want to be remembered? How would you like to be described?

> I have fought
> the good fight,
> I have finished my race,
> I have kept the faith.
> —2 Timothy 4:7

Discuss:
❖ If this is how you want to be remembered, what do you need to do now to make that happen?

Something Even Better
We all know we will one day die. Living in complete trust of God's goodness makes that a wonderful promise rather than a looming threat. Sure, we love being alive and don't want to let go of all this world offers. At the same time we also trust that God has something even better in store for us. We don't know what the next life looks like, but we do know God walks with us each step of this life even unto the next.

"Dying well" is really about living well—taking life one day at a time in a spirit of gratitude, seeking to do God's will, trusting in God's everlasting care in life and death. This is our spiritual journey: living life in faithfulness.

ehearsal

Has anyone in the group gone through the death of a loved one or a friend? If you are comfortable, tell the group about your experience. What did you learn about death? about life? Have everyone say Romans 8:35-39 together as an affirmation.

Sing together the hymn, "When We Are Living" or another song that is familiar to your group.

nvolving

What kind of ripples might (or have) come about from practicing living well so you can die well? How could your daily routine change by the transformation taking place in your soul? Discuss how you might see all areas of your life—home, school, nature, community, world, job, paying bills, and so forth—connected in a new way based on your spiritual formation journey.

> "Where, O death, is
> your victory?
> Where, O death, is
> your sting?"
> —1 Corinthians 15:55

omorrow

❏ Read Revelation 21:10-27 each day this week. How is your picture of heaven different from this image? Journal about what you imagine heaven to be.

❏ Journal about your own hopes and fears about what happens after physical death.

❏ Ask a doctor or nurse about his or her experiences with dying persons. Ask if he or she feels a person with a Christian faith faces dying differently than does someone without faith.

❏ Using paints, markers, or another medium, make a picture of how you visualize heaven.

❏ Look up Doctor Elizabeth Kubler-Ross and her writings and see what she has to say about death and dying.

❏ Keep a gratitude journal and every day write five things for which you are thankful. Praise God for giving you life abundant!

"Let your light shine before others, so that they may see your good works and give glory to your Father in heaven." —Matthew 5:16

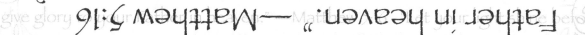

Tending Out

Last year, I attended my ten-year high school reunion in Neptune, New Jersey. After only ten years, I was amazed to see people whom I hadn't seen since graduation. Sadly, I was disheartened to find that several friends from my school Bible study no longer attended church nor tended their spiritual lives. When I asked what had happened in ten short years, the overwhelming response was that the faith that they held so closely in high school didn't seem applicable in "the real world." My friend Eric confessed, "When I was in high school it made so much sense because I was so focused on my own needs. When I got to college and beyond, I saw a church that was unwilling and unable to address real needs of hurting people in the real world." Sadly, Eric and my friends were not encouraged to practice their faith in ways that addressed those needs.

James shows us a "real world faith": "Real religion, the kind that passes muster before God the Father, is this: Reach out to the homeless and loveless in their plight, and guard against corruption from the godless world" (James 1:27, *Message*). In the same way, John Wesley preached about the need to have a faith that matched inner transformation with outward expressions. In his sermon "Advice to a People Called Methodist," John Wesley advised: "Pursue with your might inward and outward holiness; a steady imitation of Him you worship; a still increasing resemblance of his imitable perfections—his justice, mercy, and truth." In other words, make sure that neither the inner aspects nor the outward expressions of your faith become superior to the other. We do not want to become, as my grandmother would say, "so heavenly minded that we are no earthly good." At the same time, we do not want to live our lives trying to do good works that do not flow from our faith in Christ.

Tending out is the way to ensure that the fire of our inward spiritual life brings heat and light to the world around us. The life-forming practices in this section will give you life-giving ways to bear witness to the love of God that dwells in your life.

James preached that "faith by itself, if it has no works, is dead" (James 2:17) and John Wesley insisted that the true Christian life balances holiness of heart and life. In order for your life to reflect the character of Christ, your heart must be filled with the love of Christ. Offering hospitality and care or working for justice and reconciliation void of Christ's love are well-meaning acts by good people instead of life-giving acts by God's people.

Just as we are drawn to the fireplace after coming in from the cold winter air, others will be drawn to the warmth and light that comes from a spiritual fire that burns with a passionate zeal for God. Tending the embers of your soul through the inward disciplines gives heat and light to the flames that burn through the outward practices.

> Tending the embers of your soul through the inward disciplines gives heat and light to the flames that burn through the outward practices.

Almsgiving

 **Signs of the Spirit**

Discuss where you have seen God's Spirit at work this week. How have you experienced grace in a new way through Christian practice? Discuss any joys or struggles you had. How is it with your soul?

 **Purpose**

Because we long for Christ to be formed in us, we make this covenant to tend the fires of our souls so that our longing for Christ may never be extinguished and that our lives will be set ablaze with his love.

> But when you give alms, do not let your left hand know what your right hand is doing, so that your alms may be done in secret; and your Father who sees in secret will reward you.
> —Matthew 6:3-4

 **Instruction**

Although we do not usually call this practice "almsgiving," we are called to engage in it regularly as faithful Christians. Almsgiving means giving to the needy, helping the poor, taking care of those who are less fortunate, and giving yourself to the needs of others. Charity is also another way of talking about almsgiving.

❖ Are you currently in the practice of almsgiving? How?
❖ What other forms of giving might be called "almsgiving"?

John Wesley calls us to almsgiving with the right attitude. He was passionate about our doing more than just providing physical needs like shelter, food, and clothes for the poor. He felt that if one's spiritual needs are not looked after, then tending to one's physical needs is almost pointless.

In Matthew 6:1-4 Jesus teaches us what kind of givers we ought to be. To be holy as Jesus is holy, we must care for all of God's people. We must not perform acts of charity in order to look good in the eyes of others; but out of Christian love, we humbly share blessings with those in need.

❖ Have you known people who brag about giving or have you ever gloated yourself about what you have given? Discuss how hard it is to be humble in giving.

Helping those in need can be somewhat intimidating because almsgiving is not about giving what we have left over. If we do give clothes that we no longer wear, they should be gently used, not ones that are falling apart or needing repair. Almsgiving is not about getting rid of junk but reaching deeper than we thought we could go and finding something of worth to give, including even kind words at the right time.

The parable of the widow's offering in Mark 12:41-44 illustrates the attitude we should have in our almsgiving. The woman gave out of her poverty when others gave out of their wealth. She dutifully gave even when she seemingly had nothing to give.

❖ Have you ever thought that you simply did not have anything to give?

Sometimes when we do not have much money, we assume we have nothing to give. The widow clearly did not have any money, but she found money to offer. Discuss what you think this story says to us about how God sees our giving.

The story of the good Samaritan (Luke 10:25-37) tells us that not only are we to give even when we think we don't have anything, but we are also to give when it may be inconvenient. Surely stopping to help the man on the road infringed somewhat on the Samaritan's schedule, but that is the nature of almsgiving—reaching deeply into our pockets, closets, time, and energy.

In the space below, list things that you could give, then discuss your thoughts as a group.

> But she out of her poverty has put in everything she had, all she had to live on.
> —Mark 12:44b

Rehearsal

Reflect on the past week. Can you think of times when you could have been less excessive? What times did you choose to look the other way and didn't help someone in need? What times did you remain silent when someone needed to hear kind words? Discuss what it would take for you to become a more giving person. Do you hoard things or do you give freely? Do you complain about what you don't have or do you buy things to meet the needs of others? Do you give what you have left over or do you reach deeply to give extra?

nvolving

What kind of ripples might (or have) come about from practicing almsgiving? How could your daily routine change by the transformation taking place in your soul? Discuss how you might see all areas of your life—home, school, nature, community, world, job, paying bills, and so forth—connected in a new way based on your spiritual formation journey.

omorrow

❑ Go through your CD collection and take out the CD's you no longer listen to. Donate them to a youth shelter.

❑ Go to the Habitat for Humanity website (*www.habitat.org*) and request a Habitat Bank. Fill one of the cardboard houses with the change you collect. When the house is full, go to the bank and get a cashier's check and send it to Habitat for Humanity.

❑ Make a rule that every time you buy new clothes or shoes, you will give something away that you haven't worn in a year. Give the clothes or shoes to a needy friend or to a shelter.

❑ Every time you stay with a friend, go on a trip, visit relatives, or stay in a hotel, put a dollar in a box for each night you sleep away from home. You will realize you always have shelter no matter where you go. When you get enough in your box, buy a sleeping bag and pillow for a homeless shelter. Put a note of encouragement in the sleeping bag.

❑ Keep a log of how many miles you spend in a car, driving or riding. For every mile traveled, put a nickel in a jar. When the jar is full, buy gas vouchers or bus passes that the homeless shelter can use.

❑ Every time you do laundry, put a quarter in a jar. When it gets full, buy a bottle of detergent, fabric sheets, and so forth. Take your donation of laundry supplies to a domestic abuse shelter.

Evangelization and Witness

 ### igns of the Spirit

Discuss where you have seen God's Spirit at work this week. How have you experienced grace in a new way through Christian practice? Discuss any joys or struggles you had. How is it with your soul?

 ### urpose

Because we long for Christ to be formed in us, we make this covenant to tend the fires of our souls so that our longing for Christ may never be extinguished and that our lives will be set ablaze with his love.

 ### nstruction

Although to believe so is to risk stereotyping, the clothes we wear and the friends we have say a lot about us. Most of us probably don't even mind that others look at us and get a small idea of who we are. We dress and act in the way we want to present ourselves.

❖ What are some of the ways that we tell people who we are just by how we dress and act?

Beyond Door-to-Door Evangelism

Usually we want to present ourselves in such a way that people look at us and know at least something about us. Yet when it comes to witnessing to our faith in Jesus Christ, most of us experience a little anxiety. This reaction may be because most of us carry around negative stereotypes of "witnesses."

❖ What are some of the images or personality types that come to mind when you think of people who "witness" about their faith?

The truth is that none of us have to fit into a particular mold of witnessing, but we are *all* called to bear witness to the love of God in Jesus Christ. This calling is part of who we are as Christians. We don't necessarily have to wear "Jesus Saves" T-shirts, knock on doors, or hand out tracts; but we are to let others know through our actions and words that we profess faith in Christ. Our behavior needs to demonstrate the values and truths we hold dear, proclaiming to others that we believe in a God who lived among us, preaching good news to the poor, healing the sick, binding up the brokenhearted, eating with outcasts, and forgiving sinners.

Reflecting the Light of Christ

So what does it look like to be a witness? One helpful image is to think of bearing witness as reflecting God's light into the world.

> ❖ Discuss the ways in which you could reflect God's light into the world. Have you ever thought of witnessing in that way?

Keep a small round mirror in your pocket or wallet to remind you that you are called to reflect the light of God into the world.

Don't Wait Until You Are Perfect

Some of us might worry that we can't let others know that we are Christians because they will think we are hypocrites. But you don't have to be a "model" Christian to witness to Jesus Christ. Witnesses point to someone other than themselves. Daniel Migliore points out several features of the act of witness in *Faith Seeking Understanding*. The witness swears to tell the truth. Faithful witnesses are not attention-drawing. Instead, they direct attention to someone or some event distinct from themselves. The act of witnessing requires personal participation, commitment, and risk-taking. We don't have to be perfect to be witnesses. In the act of bearing witness and engaging in ministry, God changes us and our faith grows.

> You are a chosen race, a royal priesthood, a holy nation, God's own people, in order that you may proclaim the mighty acts of him who called you out of darkness and into his marvelous light.
>
> —1 Peter 2:9

Cloud of Witnesses

Thankfully, we don't have to bear witness alone. The heritage of witnessing is passed on from generation to generation. We learn from the witness of those who have gone before us, and we teach the next generation by our witness.

The Presbyterian Church (USA) catechism study teaches that the mission of the church is to bear witness to God's love for the world in Jesus Christ. The mission is lived out in all aspects of ministry from evangelism to hospitality. Bearing witness means caring for the needy whether they be homeless or our next door neighbor. The catechism teaches that we are all "the needy" because we all need a savior. This truth is the witness that is passed on: We have a savior who meets our needs.

Think of all the people who have pointed you towards the love of God. These people make up your "cloud of witnesses," spoken of in Hebrews: "Therefore, since we are surrounded by so great a cloud of witnesses, let us also lay aside every weight and the sin that clings so closely, and let us run with perseverance the race that is set before us" (Hebrews 12:1).

❖ Tell about those persons in your life who have been witnesses for you. Write in the space below what made them such great witnesses and for what you admire them most.

Mark Schultz's song, "Cloud of Witnesses," talks about the people who have helped us grow in our faith and stood beside us in our ups and downs.

❖ What are some ways that people in your church are witnesses for you?

❖ How can your group be a cloud of witnesses for one another? for the next generation?

You Will Receive Power

Sometimes we just don't feel like we are up to the job of bearing witness. Some days it seems our prayer life is in a shambles, our integrity is in question, and we aren't sure what we believe. But we are not alone. Read aloud the last words Jesus tells his disciples before his ascension into heaven: "But you will receive power when the Holy Spirit has come upon you; and you will be my witnesses in Jerusalem, in all Judea and Samaria, and to the ends of the earth" (Acts 1:8).

 ehearsal

Talk about how each member in your group has reflected God's light in the world. For example, "Sherri, you were a witness to me when you had the courage to give the children's message in worship last week." Or "Tom, you were a witness to me when I saw you helping out the new members of the team at soccer practice."

Take a minute to gather your thoughts about what your witness will be. As you feel comfortable, tell the group your faith story and talk about ways in which you could be a witness to others based on your own story. Make some notes in the space below if needed.

 nvolving

What kind of ripples might (or have) come about from practicing evangelization and witness? How could your daily routine change by the transformation taking place in your soul? Discuss how you might see all areas of your life—home, school, nature, community, world, job, paying bills, and so forth—connected in a new way based on your spiritual formation journey.

> By this everyone will know that you are my disciples, if you have love for one another.
> —John 13:35

 omorrow

❑ Volunteer to meet with a younger youth from your congregation and share some stories of your faith with him or her.

❑ Talk to a friend at school or work about how you have experienced God's love in your life.

❑ At the end of each day, consider the ways in which you have reflected the love of God in the world. Make a list in your journal of ways that you did this and also any missed opportunities.

❑ As a group, plan a "cloud of witnesses" party in your church. Invite adults and children from your congregation and the community and celebrate the ways they have been witnesses to you. Make fun invitations, serve refreshments, write and act out a skit about different ways they have been witnesses to you, giving thanks to them and to God for their ministry.

Seeking and Granting Forgiveness

 **igns of the Spirit**

Discuss where you have seen God's Spirit at work this week. How have you experienced grace in a new way through Christian practice? Discuss any joys or struggles you had. How is it with your soul?

 **urpose**

Because we long for Christ to be formed in us, we make this covenant to tend the fires of our souls so that our longing for Christ may never be extinguished and that our lives will be set ablaze with his love.

 **nstruction**

Maya spent years trying to be a Christian, but she finally gave up. "The forgiveness thing was too tough for me," she explained. "Forgiving other people sounds good on paper; but in real life, there were simply some people I could not forgive."

Maya is right. Living as a forgiven and forgiving person is a difficult aspect of the Christian faith for many people. Yet one of the beauties of the Christian faith is the simple fact that Jesus says, "Forgive, and you will be forgiven; give, and it will be given to you" (Luke 6:37-38). All of us have moments when we sin in thought, word, and deed. We commit sins by doing some things and by leaving other things undone. Therefore, it is important that we know both how to seek and how to grant others forgiveness.

As We Forgive

When Jesus taught his followers how to pray, he gave them the immediate connection between receiving forgiveness from God and granting others forgiveness. "Forgive us for doing wrong, as we forgive others" (Matthew 6:12, CEV), the Bible says. It works both ways: Forgiveness from God is connected to our own gift of forgiveness to others.

Soul-Tending: Life-Forming Practices for Older Youth & Young Adults

❖ Do you think it is harder to forgive or to ask for forgiveness? Explain your position.

So Sue Me!

We live in a society where many people, if they are angry with the actions of others, take them to court rather than offer forgiveness. That's not what Jesus had in mind! List the kinds of things that require forgiveness.

> It is by forgiving that one is forgiven.
> —Mother Teresa

How many of you can see something on this list that you have done to another person? Since we are all human, we have been on both sides of the fence.

A Right-on Parable

Read aloud the parable of the unforgiving servant in Matthew 18:23-35. Have one reader be the narrator, with other voices as the unforgiving servant (verses 26b, 28b,) other slave (29b), or king (32b-33). Why do you think Jesus told this story right after Peter asked a question about forgiveness in verse 21? What is the point of this passage?

A Radical Alternative?

Some people refuse to act in revenge and retaliation. Murder Victims' Families for Reconciliation even has a mission to abolish the death penalty. These people, all of whom have family members who were murdered, are putting their energy into working for policies and programs that reduce the rate of homicide and promote alternatives to violence. Reconciliation means accepting that you cannot undo the murder, but you can decide how you want to live afterward. Wow! Think of losing a loved one, then having the strength to forgive the murderer. Discuss:

❖ What would be the hardest things for you personally to forgive?

Then ask everyone to close their eyes as someone reads aloud Luke 23:33-34a. Have a few minutes of silence to reflect on the Scripture passage and what God might be saying to you about forgiveness.

Even as he was dying, Jesus was able to forgive those who had pierced his hands with nails and were watching him suffer. Even then he forgave. He doesn't ask us to do anything he didn't already do, and his death makes possible our own forgiveness.

 ehearsal

Look at some different translations of Matthew 6:12. How do the different wordings clarify the meaning of this verse?
    Read this prayer together:

Almighty and merciful God, you made us. You love us. You forgive us. We know all that and are grateful, yet still we fail to follow the path you have set before us. We do not live out of the fullness of your love. Instead we say and do things that hurt other people. We do not keep always before us your justice and righteousness but rather let our words and actions be governed by our own prejudices and misunderstandings. We are selfish and unsympathetic when you call us to live for others in a generous spirit. We are afraid to risk being different, fearful to speak out for truth, and not sure we can handle the consequences of following Jesus. And so we ask your forgiveness. Give us the strength to return your love with our own loving lives. Let us forgive others as we know we need to be forgiven. All things are possible in you. Amen.

 ## nvolving

What kind of ripples might (or have) come about from seeking and granting forgiveness? How could your daily routine change by the transformation taking place in your soul? Discuss how you might see all areas of your life—home, school, nature, community, world, job, paying bills, and so forth—connected in a new way based on your spiritual formation journey.

 ## omorrow

❏ Journal and/or pray about the need for forgiveness in your life.

❏ Commit to seeking forgiveness from whom you need it or granting forgiveness to those who need it from you.

❏ Reread Matthew 6:12 daily. If you say these words enough, do you think you can grow into living this message?

❏ Write your own prayer asking God for forgiveness. Think about any persons you may have hurt. Are you ready to ask them for forgiveness? If not, how can you grow toward that stage?

❏ Ask a person whom you admire and trust to share a time when he or she had trouble asking for or granting forgiveness.

Hospitality and Care

igns of the Spirit

Discuss where you have seen God's Spirit at work this week. How have you experienced grace in a new way through Christian practice? Discuss any joys or struggles you had. How is it with your soul?

urpose

Because we long for Christ to be formed in us, we make this covenant to tend the fires of our souls so that our longing for Christ may never be extinguished and that our lives will be set ablaze with his love.

nstruction

A dictionary definition of *hospitality* only begins to explain the word's meaning. Yes, hospitality is "the friendly and generous reception and entertainment of guests or strangers." However, hospitality also involves opening one's heart to all people in the spirit of Christ. Just as God gave us the earth as our wonderful home and reaches out to us in love, we are called to offer that love to everyone we meet.

You Are (Not) Welcome!

Have you ever been a guest in someone's home where you immediately felt comfortable and happy? Or have you had the opposite experience where you never quite felt "at home" in a new setting?

❖ What was it that made the difference in these two situations? What words would you use to describe people who are hospitable?

Welcoming Others

In his letters to the early church, Paul repeatedly encouraged the believers to "welcome one another, therefore, just as Christ has welcomed you, for the glory of God" (Romans 15:7). Paul was talking about more than providing a place to stay and food to eat; he meant also sharing lives and faith. As Marjorie J. Thompson writes in *Soul Feast*, "Hospitality is essentially an expression of love. It is a movement to include the guest in the very best of what we ourselves have received and can therefore offer. It is the act of sharing *who we are* as well as *what we have*."[1] Discuss ways in which we can share of ourselves, not just our things. Listed below are some different situations in which one can be hospitable (according to Thompson's definition):

- ❖ in the family (to each family member)
- ❖ in the home (to those outside your family)
- ❖ in a friendship group (to those who are not your closest friends)
- ❖ in a church congregation (to persons of a different religion)
- ❖ in the community (to people you don't know)
- ❖ in the world (to those who live far away)

Welcoming Christ

Read Matthew 25:31-40. Is Jesus clear about what he expects from his followers? Which of these situations is harder for you to think about doing: providing food, providing drink, welcoming a stranger in your home, giving clothing, caring for the sick, or visiting a prisoner? Why? Which of these situations have you helped before? How did you feel? Is it possible to do a good thing (like caring for the sick or giving clothes) without doing it in a spirit of hospitality? How?

❖ Divide into two groups and say this litany together:

GROUP 1:	I was hungry,
GROUP 2:	and you fed me.
GROUP 1:	I was thirsty,
GROUP 2:	and you gave me drink.
GROUP 1:	I was a stranger,
GROUP 2:	and you received me in your home.
GROUP 1:	I was naked,
GROUP 2:	and you clothed me.
GROUP 1:	I was sick,
GROUP 2:	and you took care of me.
GROUP 1:	I was in prison,
GROUP 2:	and you visited me.
ALL:	Just as you did it to one of the least of these who are members of my family, you did it to me.

Angels Unaware

Hebrews 13:2 says, "Do not neglect to show hospitality to strangers, for by doing that some have entertained angels without knowing it." Give an example of a time that you offered hospitality to someone and ended up feeling blessed from the experience.

The Risk of Hospitality

Look at the story of Elijah and the widow of Zarephath (1 Kings 17:8-16). Then discuss the story from the widow's perspective. What risk did she take when she offered the prophet food? How was she rewarded for her hospitality? Why do you think God brought these two people together? How does providing hospitality help us in our spiritual growth?

Soul-Tending: Life-Forming Practices for Older Youth & Young Adults

 ehearsal

Discuss how you might show hospitality to the following people:

❖ a family who moves in next door
❖ the homeless persons in your community
❖ a new student at school
❖ visitors in worship services

Is not this the fast that I choose: …to share your bread with the hungry, and bring the homeless poor into your house; when you see the naked, to cover them, and not to hide yourself from your own kin?

—Isaiah 58:6-7

 nvolving

What kind of ripples might (or have) come about from practicing hospitality and care? How could your daily routine change by the transformation taking place in your soul? Discuss how you might see all areas of your life—home, school, nature, community, world, job, paying bills, and so forth—connected in a new way based on your spiritual formation journey.

 omorrow

☐ Invite a guest to a family dinner.

☐ Talk with your family about possible ways to provide hospitality. You might consider hosting a holiday meal for people who don't have nearby family, hosting a foreign exchange student, inviting persons who live alone to join you on family activities, organizing a block party, and so forth.

☐ Journal about any inner roadblocks for you concerning hospitality. What holds you back from fully opening your heart in the spirit of Christ?

☐ When have you "met" Jesus in another person? Reflect on how you can show Jesus to others through hospitality.

Notes
[1] Reprinted from *Soul Feast: An Invitation to the Christian Spiritual Life* by Marjorie J. Thompson. © 1995 Marjorie J. Thompson. Used by permission.

Stewardship of Household Economics and Money

igns of the Spirit

Discuss where you have seen God's Spirit at work this week. How have you experienced grace in a new way through Christian practice? Discuss any joys or struggles you had. How is it with your soul?

> For where your treasure is, there your heart will be also.
> —Matthew 6:21

urpose

Because we long for Christ to be formed in us, we make this covenant to tend the fires of our souls so that our longing for Christ may never be extinguished and that our lives will be set ablaze with his love.

nstruction

The fact that Jesus said more about money than about any other temporal subject is convincing evidence that he saw our relationship to money as a spiritual issue. Remember that he was speaking to people in a simple society where land was a highly valued asset. What would he have to say to us who live in a world of high technology, great material wealth, and seemingly endless ways to spend money?

Need or Want?

Write a list of the things you think are important in life. Then mark what you actually *need in order to survive.* How many of us have all that we actually need, even if we do not have all we want?

Start With the Basics

Let's look at some of the ways Jesus addressed the subject of finances and possessions. Discuss how you would describe Jesus' attitude towards wealth. Take turns reading the following passages: Luke 6:20, 24; Luke 12:15; and Luke 16:13. Compare those passages with what you said about Jesus' attitude towards wealth.

❖ Do you have any new insights after reading the Scripture?

Bigger Barns

Living in a prosperous nation can be seductive. Most of us can find other people who have more possessions than we do. If nothing else, we may subconsciously compare ourselves to the movie stars or professional athletes who own multimillion-dollar homes, numerous cars, and have a stock portfolio bigger than the budget of a small city. "I don't have so many things," we tell ourselves. "It won't hurt to buy one more CD, one more sweater, or one more pair of jeans." Being content is not a matter of more as much as of enough. When are we satisfied with our possessions and thinking we have enough stuff? Read the parable of the rich fool from Luke 12:13-21.

In pairs, discuss these questions:

❖ How do I build bigger barns on earth?

❖ How am I storing treasures in heaven?

> Each of you must give as you have made up your mind, not reluctantly or under compulsion, for God loves a cheerful giver.
>
> —2 Corinthians 9:7

Rethinking Possessions

Richard Foster, writing about simplicity, gives some practical ideas for how to not be sucked into the consumer society but rather, to keep our focus on "treasure in heaven." Here are some of his suggestions:

❖ Buy useful things, not trendy things.
❖ Reject addictions.
❖ Regularly clean out your closets and give away what you don't use.
❖ Avoid being wooed by commercials.
❖ Enjoy things instead of possessing them.
❖ Deepen your awareness of God's good creation.
❖ Turn from whatever keeps you focused on your goal.

In small groups talk about Foster's suggestions. Which of these ideas rings a bell in your own life?

Giving From Our Own Abundance

If we compare our own lives to that of an Afghani refugee, Salvadorean orphan, or a homeless person in Chicago, we have to admit that we have it pretty good. One of the gifts of having enough (or more than enough) is that we can then give from our abundance to others. As Paul wrote in 2 Corinthians 9:8 and 11a, "And God is able to provide you with every blessing in abundance, so that by always having enough of everything, you may share abundantly in every good work. You will be enriched in every way for your great generosity . . ."

Giving helps others and makes us feel good. Giving as an act of worship is what God calls us to do. We give because we want to honor God and share God's love. Brainstorm some of the ways that you can give to help others by making monetary donations or giving of your time and energy. What can you do as individuals or a group?

Tithing and Regular Giving

When we think about the fact that everything we have comes from God, it should cause us to want to give back to God a portion of what we have been generously given. This issue is not simply a matter of economics; it is a spiritual one. Tithing is our act of obedience to God's command of giving ten percent of what we have to God. Offerings go above and beyond this call to an act of worship and gratitude.

When a person sets aside a portion of what he or she earns or receives through an allowance, that person is saying, "God is more important in my life than money. Tithing and giving regular offerings are ways of worshiping and saying, 'Thank you for all I have.'" For many, putting their cash or check into an offering envelope is a part of their ongoing spiritual journey. "I put God first," says one young person. "Even if there's another bill I can't pay in full, my tithe goes to God's work. It's so little compared to all that God has done for me.'"

 ehearsal

Make three columns and mark them as "Real Treasure," "Nice to Have," and "Can Live Without." Then read the following list and write each item in the appropriate column for your own life. This exercise is a personal assessment, not a "right or wrong" test: education, family, car, good health, large screen television, surround sound, adequate spending money, enough food to eat, an in-style wardrobe, friends, God's love, peace of mind, church family, a place to live, access to medical care, creativity, CD player, access to a library, church youth group, fraternity or sorority membership, musical or physical talent, intelligence, and popularity.

Examine your own life. Add to these columns from your personal situation.

In pairs, compare lists and discuss why you placed each item in its column. Come back together as a group and discuss, what are the most important treasures in your life? Read aloud together Matthew 6:19-21.

 nvolving

What kind of ripples might (or have) come about from practicing stewardship of household economics and money? How could your daily routine change by the transformation taking place in your soul? Discuss how you might see all areas of your life—home, school, nature, community, world, job, paying bills, and so forth—connected in a new way based on your spiritual formation journey.

 omorrow

❑ Imagine that a great fire or flood is moving toward your home. You have ten minutes to gather together a few things before you must evacuate. What will you take? Make a list; then write in your journal about why each of these items is important to you. Why is it worth saving? What makes it valuable to you?

❑ Spend fifteen minutes each day this week thanking God for all your treasures or make a list of thirty things for which you are thankful.

❑ Each day this week, read the story of the rich young man who came to Jesus from Matthew 19:16-24. Imagine what might have happened in that young man's life after his encounter with Jesus. Can you write a new ending to the story?

❑ Keep track this week of every expense, including even the smallest amount spent. As you look over where your money goes, pray that God would show you how to be faithful with your money. Listen for God's speaking to you about money this week. Then create a budget that reflects your insight.

❑ Think about your own life. When and how have you been "a cheerful giver"?

❑ Ask your parents or other significant adults about their giving practices.

Stewardship of Creation and Time

 ## igns of the Spirit

Discuss where you have seen God's Spirit at work this week. How have you experienced grace in a new way through Christian practice? Discuss any joys or struggles you had. How is it with your soul?

> The earth is the LORD's and all that is in it, the world, and those who live in it …
> —Psalm 24:1

 ## urpose

Because we long for Christ to be formed in us, we make this covenant to tend the fires of our souls so that our longing for Christ may never be extinguished and that our lives will be set ablaze with his love.

 ## nstruction

Called to Stewardship

A good steward is one who takes special care to use all things wisely. One can be a steward of money and use it well in saving, spending, and giving. We are good stewards of the earth when we strive to keep it clean and care for all creation in a way that will help it to last. Stewardship of time involves how we use the moments given to us in our lives.

Brother Sun, Sister Moon

In the twelfth century, Saint Francis of Assisi communed with nature. He used new images for parts of creation: "Brother Sun," "Sister Moon," "Brother Wind," and "Mother Earth." They showed the close connection Francis felt with nature. Imagine that every flower whose beauty you admire, every mountain you climb, each animal you see is a relative—brother, sister, or cousin. Would you act differently if you thought your family was being trampled, polluted, or made extinct? How can we capture that feeling of connection to nature so we personally care for all creation?

Soul-Tending: Life-Forming Practices for Older Youth & Young Adults

Stewardship of the Earth

Read Genesis 1:26-31, then discuss:

❖ What was God's reaction to what God had made?

❖ What do you think God meant by saying that humans would "have dominion" over the earth and its creatures (verses 26 and 28)?

❖ Read verses 29-31a. How does this show the interrelatedness of all creatures? Given these words, what responsibility do humans have in caring for the earth?

A Vision of Doom

Have someone read aloud Isaiah 24:4-5. How do these verses describe what has happened in our contemporary world? How can we apply the words "they have transgressed laws, violated the statutes, broken the everlasting covenant" to the destruction of the earth in our time?

Where Do You Stand?

In the past decade, environmental action has come to the forefront of our consciousness. Public education on the ozone layer, water pollution, and the effects of chemicals on the land have increased greatly. Many cities now have curbside recycling. Yet Americans still consume at an unrelenting rate, landfills are overflowing, and problems with pollution of all kinds persist. In pairs discuss what you do to care for the earth, then come together as a group and compile your list of items below as a future resource for action.

❖ God gives each of us not only the gift of life but also the beautiful world in which we live. How can we see those actions we take for the environmental health of the world as part of our own spiritual journey?

> The high,
> the low
> all of creation,
> God gives to
> humankind to use. If
> this privilege is misused,
> God's Justice permits
> creation to punish
> humanity.
> —Hildegard of Bingen

Stewardship of Time

God is in all our moments. How does that truth make an impact upon the way you use your time? Journal in response to these questions:

❖ In which of my daily activities am I most conscious of God?
❖ What things do I do each day to acknowledge God's presence in my life?

 ehearsal

Sing "For the Beauty of the Earth," "God of the Sparrow," "All Things Bright and Beautiful," or another creation-centered hymn or song.

Say together this prayer: God of heaven and earth, Teach us the true beauty of your creation. Teach us what it means to have dominion over the earth that you created for us. Give us the wisdom to care for the earth and keep our time well.

> Dost thou love life? Then do not squander time, for that is the stuff life is made of.
> —Benjamin Franklin

 nvolving

What kind of ripples might (or have) come about from practicing stewardship of creation and time? How could your daily routine change by the transformation taking place in your soul? Discuss how you might see all areas of your life—home, school, nature, community, world, job, paying bills, and so forth—connected in a new way based on your spiritual formation journey.

 omorrow

❑ Brainstorm how you can increase your conscious behavior in applying the "three r's" (reuse, reduce, recycle) in your daily life. Make a pledge to change one behavior. For instance, if you drink one soda each day and presently throw the can in the trash, promise yourself that you will find and use a recycle bin for aluminum. Or you might recycle paper you have written on to use the other side for note paper.

❑ In your journal, answer these questions:
  ❖ In what sense is my time not just my own, but God's?
  ❖ What can I do each day to give my time to God?
  ❖ Does my current use of time show that God is a priority in my life?

❑ Look for an environmental group with whom you can work—either an on-campus club, a local group, or a national organization.

❑ Go online and investigate the current state of environmental problems in the world at *actionnetwork.org*.

Acts of Justice and Reconciliation

 **igns of the Spirit**

Discuss where you have seen God's Spirit at work this week. How have you experienced grace in a new way through Christian practice? Discuss any joys or struggles you had. How is it with your soul?

 **urpose**

Because we long for Christ to be formed in us, we make this covenant to tend the fires of our souls so that our longing for Christ may never be extinguished and that our lives will be set ablaze with his love.

> Love cannot remain by itself—it has no meaning. Love has to be put into action and that action is service.
> —Mother Teresa

 **nstruction**

Who Is My Neighbor?

Read the story of the good Samaritan in Luke 10:25-37, then discuss:

❖ Why did Jesus tell this story in response to the question, "And who is my neighbor"?
❖ In today's world, who is your neighbor?
❖ What are some of the ways you can come to the aid of your neighbors?

Justice, Mercy, Kindness

Read the following biblical passages to get some ideas as to how God wants us to respond to others' needs: Psalm 33:4-5; Psalm 89:14; Psalm 146:5-10; Proverbs 21:3; Amos 5:24; and Micah 6:8. What common themes do you find?

Each person must find his or her own ways to act out God's call to do justice. What are you doing? Brainstorm more ways you can be of service. What about a work day building with Habitat for Humanity or an evening serving food at a soup kitchen? Go further: Learn about the root causes of homelessness, hunger, poverty, or another area of need that cries out for justice and reconciliation.

Now list some ways that you could work for justice through bringing about social change. Is there a local issue you could research and perhaps educate the public, circulate a petition, or find some other way to work for justice?

Works of Justice, Works of Mercy

Loving our neighbor means more than providing direct help. Our love may also mean trying to change the circumstances that keep our neighbor in need. Working for justice can take on many forms. Look also for little things that you can incorporate into your life to bring about change. List some ways that you could work for justice through acts of mercy.

❖ In assessing your individual and group activities, would you say you spend more of your time on yourself or working for mercy and justice for others?

❖ What could you do to bring that effort more into balance?

Reconciliation

Acts of reconciliation can be large such as President Jimmy Carter's bringing together Israel's Menachim Begin and Egypt's Anwar Sadat for the Mideast Peace Accords. They can also be small, such as one teenager's acting as a mediator to help two friends hear each other's feelings.

Paul said, "So if anyone is in Christ, there is a new creation: everything old has passed away; see, everything has become new! All this is from God, who reconciled us to himself through Christ, and has given us the ministry of reconciliation; that is, in Christ God was reconciling the world to himself, not counting their trespasses against them, and entrusting the message of reconciliation to us. So we are ambassadors for Christ ..."(2 Corinthians 5:17-20). For some of us, this ambassadorship may mean sharing the good news about Jesus with other people. For others it may mean seeing yourself as a peacemaker who, because you know Jesus, seeks to bring people together in harmony whenever possible. Reread Paul's words above and think about how you might participate in acts of reconciliation.

 ehearsal

What people in your church or community are active in works of justice, mercy, or reconciliation? How could they help you get started?

Divide the space below into three columns: works of justice, works of mercy, and acts of reconciliation. Write down things you are currently doing in each category and then what you would like to try doing. Discuss your lists.

nvolving

What kind of ripples might (or have) come about from practicing acts of justice and reconciliation? How could your daily routine change by the transformation taking place in your soul? Discuss how you might see all areas of your life—home, school, nature, community, world, job, paying bills, and so forth—connected in a new way based on your spiritual formation journey.

> What does the LORD require of you but to do justice, and to love kindness, and to walk humbly with your God?
> —Micah 6:8

omorrow

❑ Thoroughly read the newspaper at least one day this week. Is there any situation where people are hurting about which you might be able to do something? Write letters to governmental representatives, donate money or other necessary items, educate yourself so you can help others understand why people need help, or join a group that is working on the issue; be creative in finding ways to give of yourself.

❑ Do some research on Jimmy Carter and his commitment to peace in the Middle East or his work to make housing affordable and available. How do you think his commitment to Jesus Christ has influenced his work?

❑ Commit to being a peacemaker this week.

❑ Investigate ways you can learn to transform conflict. Check and visit the website for JUSTPEACE at *www.JUSTPEACEumc.org*.

Confessing to One Another

Signs of the Spirit

Discuss where you have seen God's Spirit at work this week. How have you experienced grace in a new way through Christian practice? Discuss any joys or struggles you had. How is it with your soul?

Purpose

Because we long for Christ to be formed in us, we make this covenant to tend the fires of our souls so that our longing for Christ may never be extinguished and that our lives will be set ablaze with his love.

> Confess your sins to one another, and pray for one another, so that you may be healed. The prayer of the righteous is powerful and effective.
> —James 5:16

Instruction

Have you ever been face-to-face with your own failure or inadequacy? When have you had to honestly acknowledge the wrong-doing in your life? Would you dare trust another believer with the secrets of your sin? Confessing shines a light on our fear, hatred, anxiety, and all our obsessions—the clutter of sin. It sweeps away the debris and makes room for God to live more fully in our hearts. Discuss what you think of when you hear the word *confession*.

❖ What things might one need to confess?

❖ Have you ever had to make a confession?

Giving Confession

We are all so human. Confessing our sin to another is not easy to do. We want to be right; we want others to think well of us, and we want to feel good about ourselves. However, when sin stays in our hearts, we don't feel good about ourselves, and our wrong-doings tear away at our relationships with others and with God. Discuss the following questions:

Soul-Tending: Life-Forming Practices for Older Youth & Young Adults

❖ When have you tried to hide the fact that you needed to make a confession?

❖ Have you ever tried to convince yourself that you were right, even when you knew otherwise? When?

God's amazing love helps us to confess. God knows the facts of our sin. Yet God loves us so much that God sent the Savior to release us from that sin. Confessing causes us to accept the reality of our sin. But confession also clears away the garbage in our hearts and makes straight again the path to loving one another and God.

Receiving Confession

When we are on the receiving end of confession, we hold a sacred trust. The person making confession has stopped pretending, stopped hiding behind an "ideal" self, and become more transparent. What is our role in this time of his or her vulnerability? As we listen, we are able to catch a glimpse of our true selves and the reality of our own humanness. We are not in a position to judge another.

We are to bear one another's burdens and suffer alongside their pain. We humbly speak the truth and courageously listen with compassion and love. Along with the one making confession, we give the need to God. And we continue our prayers for the wholeness of the other.

With a partner discuss these questions:

❖ What do giving and receiving confession have to do with your spiritual life or your relationship with God?

❖ Is confessing to another believer necessary? Why not just confess to God? How might making confession to another human being be important?

❖ How might giving confession mold you more and more into the image of God that you were created to be?

❖ How might receiving confession mold you more and more into the image of God that you were created to be?

❖ What's the connection between the practice of confession and a strong community of faith?

Rehearsal

Talk in pairs. One person gives and the other receives the confession. Take a few minutes to prepare. The one giving the confession needs to speak the truth about the sin in his or her life. The receiver is called to listen with compassion and lay the need before God—fixing and judging is God's business.

Trade confessor roles with your partner. After the time of confession, spend a few minutes debriefing the experience. Write any insights or thoughts below.

Involving

What kind of ripples might (or have) come about from confessing to one another? How could your daily routine change by the transformation taking place in your soul? Discuss how you might see all areas of your life—home, school, nature, community, world, job, paying bills, and so forth—connected in a new way based on your spiritual formation journey.

Tomorrow

❑ Put five different sized and shaped beads on a cord. Develop an easy prayer guide to correspond with the beads. Perhaps the first bead will remind you of the call to confession and prayer in James 5:16. The next might cue a time of silent confession. The middle bead might signal a time of listening for God. The fourth might lead you to pray your way into the life of another for whom you have a concern. Let the last bead signal the praying of the Lord's Prayer. Carry the prayer beads in your pocket and use them for God's loving purpose.

❑ Find and cultivate a relationship with someone with whom you can confess.

❑ Read Luke 15:11-32, the parable of the lost son, each day this week. Reflect on what you learned in this session, especially as you consider both the younger and the older son. Is there a relationship in your life that might be brought under God's gaze? Initiate the giving or receiving of confession, as is fitting.

❑ Pray prayers of intercession on a regular basis. Ask God to supply the needs of others, especially that they might be able to let go of the clutter of sin in their lives and make room for God to live more fully in their hearts. Set aside times for prayer each day. Cycle prayers according to the days of the week. Pray by name for family members one day. Pray for your instructors or friends from work, name by name, another day. Hold your classmates or roommates in prayer on yet another day. Choose another day to focus on those for whom you have concern. Ask others, "How should I pray for you?"

Prophetic Witness

 ## igns of the Spirit

Discuss where you have seen God's Spirit at work this week. How have you experienced grace in a new way through Christian practice? Discuss any joys or struggles you had. How is it with your soul?

 ## urpose

Because we long for Christ to be formed in us, we make this covenant to tend the fires of our souls so that our longing for Christ may never be extinguished and that our lives will be set ablaze with his love.

 ## nstruction

Are you puzzled, challenged, or even angered by what is going on in the world? Do you wonder why there seems to be such a huge gap between the world that God intended and the way things really are? Do you ever find yourself asking God to intervene to change the course of history or to bring about peace, justice, and righteousness? Do you ever sense that God is speaking through you?

"Thus Says the Lord"

In the Bible, prophets are those who speak God's Word to a present situation. They are in tune with the events of their time—warfare, poverty, worship of false gods, and complacency—and they are also open to the will of God. The perception that prophets "predict the future" is only partially true. Prophets are given a vision that has implications for the present and the future.

In the Old Testament, the books written by the prophets are the second major portion of Scripture, following the Law. Prophets like Isaiah, Jeremiah, and Ezekiel called the people to follow God's Law, to remember God's salvation, to accept God's judgment, and to receive God's mercy. They did this by making the word of God plain ("thus says the Lord") and also by pointing others to signs. Jeremiah spoke of a potter working with clay, which teaches us that God shapes and molds us for a variety of purposes. Ezekiel envisioned a valley of dry bones, which reminds us that God can bring life out of death.

Two Evils and One Kingdom

The prophetic words are always vivid and stark; they get our attention! The prophets spoke chiefly against two evils: our tendency to worship other gods and our neglect of the poor. They spoke to the complacent and self-sufficient, warning them of coming disaster. They spoke to people in exile, driven from their homes, assuring them of protection.

Also, in their own time and today, the prophets envision a reality that is so different from what we know that we are forced to look and listen. Isaiah spoke of the wolf lying down with the lamb in a vision of the "peaceable kingdom." In a world marked by war, violence, and conflict, God's vision for the world is given to us by the prophets, and we are called to live toward that vision.

Martin Luther King, Jr., was a prophetic witness in the last century. He reminded people of the difference between their public profession ("that all are created equal") and their practice in regard to people of other races. He called Christians back to listen to the prophets. One of his favorite Scriptures was Amos 5:24: "Let justice roll down like waters, and righteousness like an ever-flowing stream." In this way, his voice was in the tradition of the prophets of ancient Israel.

> Let justice roll down like waters, and righteousness like an ever-flowing stream.
> —Amos 5:24

❖ What are the prophetic voices in your own community?

Today's Prophets

You may have heard that the role of the prophet is to afflict the comfortable and comfort the afflicted. To those who are comfortable and complacent, the prophets bring a warning. To those who are suffering and burdened, the prophets bring a word of hope.

❖ Who are the comfortable in your community?

❖ Who are the afflicted in your community?

Someone wrote to the local newspaper in my community, "I notice people are constantly quoting the Bible to condemn other people. Here is a verse that I will offer to the community." Then he quoted from the teaching of Jesus: "Whoever has two coats must share with anyone who has none; and whoever has food must do likewise"(Luke 3:11). This simple reminder was a prophetic witness. Many of us have more than one coat. Many others have none. Through this man's witness some were afflicted, others comforted.

❖ What would a prophetic witness sound like in your community?

❖ What issues, problems, or concerns would be addressed?

❖ How has the meaning of prophecy been misunderstood in these days of psychic networks and end-time predictions?

❖ How do you identify a true prophecy? How do you test it?

Young persons have always been at the forefront of the church's prophetic witness in the world. You often come to the Word of God with a freshness, and you are skilled in seeing how the Word might connect with the world. Listen to the prophets! They are speaking to you, and they can also speak through you.

ehearsal

Why do we avoid or shy away from those who are prophets in our time? Can you think of someone in your community or church who is always saying things that go "against the grain"? What issue in your community or in the world bothers you or keeps you awake at night? What would your community look like if God's vision for it were to become a reality? Discuss the ways in which your group could be a prophetic witness in your community.

> To another [is] given [the gift of] prophecy . . . All these [gifts] are activated by one and the same Spirit, who allots to each one individually just as the Spirit chooses.
> —1 Corinthians 12:10-11

nvolving

What kind of ripples might (or have) come about from practicing prophetic witnessing? How could your daily routine change by the transformation taking place in your soul? Discuss how you might see all areas of your life—home, school, nature, community, world, job, paying bills, and so forth—connected in a new way based on your spiritual formation journey.

omorrow

❑ Read the book of Amos this week. How is his prophetic voice a witness for you today? How will his words inspire you to act?

❑ Who in your community reminds you of the Old Testament prophets? Send that person a note of encouragement.

❑ When situations or comments arise that cause some moral tension for you this week, speak up. Journal about your experiences.

Singing From the Soul

 **igns of the Spirit**

Discuss where you have seen God's Spirit at work this week. How have you experienced grace in a new way through Christian practice? Discuss any joys or struggles you had. How is it with your soul?

 **urpose**

Because we long for Christ to be formed in us, we make this covenant to tend the fires of our souls so that our longing for Christ may never be extinguished and that our lives will be set ablaze with his love.

 **nstruction**

Do you sing in the shower? How about when you're alone in your car? Do you shout your song as if the road were your stage? Consider the special occasions that prompt singing: weddings, funerals, worship services, family rituals, cultural rituals, athletic events, military workouts, as a memorization aid, or even to go to sleep. Music is also an integral part of everyday life. Somehow feelings often come with much more clarity and profoundness when they are sung. In the same way, music has the potential to draw a person closer and closer to the heart of God. A person's theology, or the way in which one thinks or studies about God, often becomes clearer and more meaningful in song.

> I will sing of your steadfast love, O LORD, forever; with my mouth I will proclaim your faithfulness to all generations. I declare that your steadfast love is established forever; your faithfulness is as firm as the heavens.
>
> —Psalm 89: 1-2

The Music We Make

Talk as a group about how singing takes place in your various worship settings. Do you sing a liturgy? chant recitatively with the priest or pastor? sing the psalms? sing hymns or praise choruses?

❖ What is your experience during the music in church? Do you enjoy or dread the music in church?

Finding Your Voice

Do you think you can sing? Are you good at playing an instrument? How can persons sing from the soul if they do not think themselves good singers? Did you know that God hears beautiful music when our songs are directed towards heaven? Have someone read aloud the verses from Psalm 89. Could you sing of God's love forever? How? Write your thoughts or insights below.

> Have an eye to God in every word you sing.
> —John Wesley

Brother Roger, the founder of the Taizé community, says that when the high point of our time with God is the kind of singing that lingers in our hearts during times of solitude, we are in true communion with God.

In a few moments of quiet, listen to the song in your heart. What are the words your heart is singing as you still your mind and listen in? Write the words below.

So what has singing to do with forming your spiritual life or your relationship with God? Why would an intentional effort to experience God's grace in music be important to your faith? When singing, a person's thoughts and reason relax, leaving an openness in the soul where the human heart is free to lean in ever so closely to the heart of God. In addition to nearing our hearts toward God, Martin Luther suggests that God's Word is instilled in us as we sing to God.

❖ What would it mean for our faith lives to have our hearts leaned into God's heart? How could God's Word be instilled in us when we sing?

John Wesley, the founder of Methodism, urges, "Have an eye to God in every word you sing." Turn to your neighbor and discuss this quotation from Wesley. After a few minutes talk as a group about the following questions:

❖ How would one "turn an eye to God" while singing?

❖ What about listening to or singing songs that aren't sung in church, such as your favorite popular CD's, radio hits, and other music you enjoy? As you or your heart sings along to the music, do you move closer to God?

❖ What does it mean to sing from the soul? Think about God's hearing your heart's song even when you're completely silent. How do you experience God's grace in the music there?

 ## ehearsal

❖ Choose a melody to sing a psalm to over and over. Then have a time of silence to listen for the melody in your heart.

❖ Think of a favorite hymn or song that expresses your love for God and sing it as a group.

❖ Chant Revelation 4:8b on one note: "Day and night without ceasing they sing, 'Holy, holy, holy is the Lord God Almighty, who was and is and is to come. Holy, holy, holy is the Lord God Almighty, who was and is and is to come. Holy, holy, holy is the Lord God Almighty, who was and is and is to come.'"

 ## nvolving

What kind of ripples might (or have) come about from singing from the soul? How could your daily routine change by the transformation taking place in your soul? Discuss how you might see all areas of your life—home, school, nature, community, world, job, paying bills, and so forth—connected in a new way based on your spiritual formation journey.

 ## omorrow

❑ Take note of your heart's song throughout the week. Journal every day about the song your heart sings.

❑ Commit to singing wholeheartedly in church this Sunday. Pray the hymns and choruses as you sing them in worship. Listen to the choir or praise team and let their songs linger in your heart.

❑ Write a song this week about your love for God.

❑ Listen to a different kind of music each day this week and listen for ways in which God speaks to you through music.

Speaking the Truth in Love

 ## igns of the Spirit

Discuss where you have seen God's Spirit at work this week. How have you experienced grace in a new way through Christian practice? Discuss any joys or struggles you had. How is it with your soul?

> Let your word be "Yes, Yes" or "No, No"; anything more than this comes from the evil one.
> —Matthew 5:37

 ## urpose

Because we long for Christ to be formed in us, we make this covenant to tend the fires of our souls so that our longing for Christ may never be extinguished and that our lives will be set ablaze with his love.

 ## nstruction

Do you ever "beat around the bush" or put up a smoke screen with the words you choose to speak? How many times have you walked away from a conversation and wondered what the other person really had on his or her mind? How often do you say what you think somebody else wants to hear? Do you ever get into trouble by saying one thing and doing the opposite?

Imagine it's December and a friend asks you to help recruit a day's worth of Salvation Army red kettle bell-ringers. You want to say yes to this good cause but really need to say no. You talk awhile to keep up appearances, offer a few excuses, and try to say no without really using the word *no*. You walk away thinking you've gotten away with a no. Then three days later, your friend calls and asks you for the names. You've got a problem—a spiritual problem.

Yes, Yes or No, No

Talk as a group about your own "red kettle" situations. Tell about a time when someone asked you to do something important. Did you beat around the bush or avoid answering all together? Did your tongue and your actions match? Or did you say yes with your tongue and no with your actions? Could you have said no without making excuses?

Soul-Tending: Life-Forming Practices for Older Youth & Young Adults

The Devil Made Me Do It

If our tongue is trying to help us make a good impression, we might get caught telling half-truths or choosing words that baffle. We might be heard giving only some of the facts or talking gibberish. Does this scenario sound familiar to you? Others can influence us as well. What happened the last time you faced a serious moral yes or no situation? Talk to a partner about who or what motivated your yes or no in that situation. Were your words true to your core values and beliefs?

What does speaking the truth in love have to do with your spiritual life and your relationship with God? What does letting your yes be yes and your no be no (James 5:12) have to do with your faith? What's the difference between looking good and being good? Our story of redemption is about a loving God who makes and keeps promises. We follow a Savior who speaks truth that gives light and helps our understanding. Our call is to make God's faithfulness known and God's love real in our world.

Plain and Honest

Truth-speaking is plain and honest talk that, like Jesus, we do not speak on our own (John 12:49). Language is a blessing from God and should be used to praise God and build up others with God's love. Discuss what it might mean to speak only in response to heavenly promptings. What might your friends and family notice about the pace of your response? the amount of words you use? your choice of words? the way you steer conversations? the relationship between what you say and do? Write any notes in the space below.

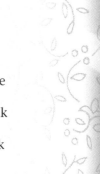

> We must no longer be children, tossed to and fro and blown about by every wind of doctrine, by people's trickery, by their craftiness in deceitful scheming. But speaking the truth in love, we must grow up in every way into him who is the head, into Christ.
>
> —Ephesians 4:14-15

Paul's letter to the Ephesians claims speaking the truth in love as a part of active spiritual service in the body of Christ. What would it mean for our faith if we spoke words that were meant to be taken at face value and rejected sarcasm or talk that flatters, hides, mocks, or confuses? What if we really accepted the power of truth-speaking to ease the tossing and blowing about of which Paul speaks? Think to yourself and write your thoughts below.

 ehearsal

Use these scenarios to role play what you might say in different situations:

❖ You are out with friends and somebody starts to gossip.
❖ Your boss asks you about some missing money.
❖ Someone asks you for a date, but you don't want to go.
❖ A regional convenience store chain offers the lowest gas prices in town. This company marks up the price of basic food items (not just candy and soda!) to recoup the profit lost on gas sales. That seems wrong to you, so you don't buy gas at these stores. You drive past the low prices and pull up to a pump a few miles down the road. A friend in the car wonders out loud about your choice.

 nvolving

What kind of ripples might (or have) come about from speaking the truth in love? How could your daily routine change by the transformation taking place in your soul? Discuss how you might see all areas of your life—home, school, nature, community, world, job, paying bills, and so forth—connected in a new way based on your spiritual formation journey.

 omorrow

❑ Develop a three-question "system" that you can use to help decide whether to say yes or no to something. The questions should help you make sure you understand what is really being asked of you (including time and energy) and how it fits with your core values and beliefs. Use your system!

❑ Write a story or picture book for children about the difference between looking good and being good.

❑ Keep a yes and no log for forty-eight hours. How many times did you let your yes be yes and your no be no? How many times did you turn your yes into a no or a no into a yes?

❑ Seek to tell the truth in everything. Be on the look-out for half-truths, expressions that flatter, sarcasm, and other opportunities to sidestep the truth.

Spiritual Direction

igns of the Spirit

Discuss where you have seen God's Spirit at work this week. How have you experienced grace in a new way through Christian practice? Discuss any joys or struggles you had. How is it with your soul?

urpose

Because we long for Christ to be formed in us, we make this covenant to tend the fires of our souls so that our longing for Christ may never be extinguished and that our lives will be set ablaze with his love.

nstruction

Whether it is learning to play the guitar, paint in oils, speak a new language, or perfect skateboard tricks, any new venture requires our energy and commitment. Having a coach can help. So it is with the spiritual life, as well. If we feel ready to go deeper, learn more, and draw closer to God, we must make time to learn and grow in God. For many people, a relationship with a spiritual director enhances their spiritual growth.

> Spiritual direction … is essentially the relationship of a teacher and learner in the area of practicing the spiritual life.
> —Marjorie J. Thompson, *Soul Feast* [1]

What Is Spiritual Direction?

Marjorie J. Thompson writes in *Soul Feast*, "Spiritual direction is basically the guidance one Christian offers another to help that person 'grow up in every way … into Christ' (Eph. 4:15). A spiritual guide is someone who can help us see and name our own experience of God."[2] The job of the spiritual director is not to pass judgment on another's spiritual journey nor to tell the directee what to do or how to fix his or her problems. Rather, a good spiritual director is above all a careful listener who offers a safe space for the other person to look deeply at his or her life. The director will encourage the directee to recognize and respond to God's presence in daily life. The director and directee may read Scripture or pray together.

What Would We Talk About?

To prepare for an initial meeting with a spiritual director, take an inventory of where you are on the spiritual path. For instance, you may say, "I go to worship and youth group or campus fellowship, but I don't know how to pray. I would read the Bible, but it doesn't make sense to me. Yet I still feel that God is in my life." You need to be open, honest, and ready to share parts of your life that you may not usually tell other people. You can be sure that your spiritual director will protect your confidentiality; whatever you say will stay between the two of you.

You may want to prepare for ongoing meetings by identifying important events in your life since the last meeting. What was the substance of your everyday life? Where did you see God? How have you acted out your faith? Your director will know good questions to ask to help you put your life into perspective and may offer suggestions of spiritual disciplines for you to try between your meetings.

Tough Questions

In the space below, write down one or two questions that you would like to discuss with a spiritual director. Read all of your questions and discuss possible answers as a group.

The conversation you had about your tough questions is similar to what a conversation with a spiritual director might be. You will wrestle together with the hard things and with the not-so-hard issues that come into your life.

❖ Have you had friends in the past with whom you could discuss the hard questions of faith? What was that like?

❖ Why would someone need this kind of relationship?

 ehearsal

Read Acts 8:26-40. How did Philip act as a spiritual guide for the Ethiopian eunuch? What traits did each of these men have that led to a positive spiritual encounter?

Pray this prayer aloud together:

> Loving God, you know us better than we know ourselves. You understand that we want to be faithful to your call, but sometimes we get distracted. We have so many other things to think about! Yet we realize that even when we forget you, you remember us and offer your love.
>
> Gracious God, help us to make you a priority in our lives. Let us strive to know you better and see if we can build on that. If we need a spiritual director, help us seek and find someone with whom to meet. Walk beside us as we journey. In Christ's name we pray, Amen.

 nvolving

What kind of ripples might (or have) come about from seeking spiritual direction? How could your daily routine change by the transformation taking place in your soul? Discuss how you might see all areas of your life—home, school, nature, community, world, job, paying bills, and so forth—connected in a new way based on your spiritual formation journey.

 omorrow

❑ Think about if you are ready to enter into a relationship with a spiritual director. If you are, then talk to your pastor or youth pastor about possible directors at nearby retreat centers or churches. If your pastor or youth pastor feels comfortable and equipped for the role, he or she might also be a good choice as spiritual director. An older man or woman, mature in the faith, may also serve in this role.

❑ Read John 3:1-6 each day this week as you reflect on finding a spiritual director. Remember that Nicodemus was a learned man of religion, yet something drew him to Jesus by dark of night. How did Nicodemus show openness to Jesus? How did Jesus mentor Nicodemus in the faith?

❑ In your life, who have been spiritual mentors or guides for you? Write each of them a thank-you letter this week and pray for them as you mail the letters.

Notes
[1] Reprinted from *Soul Feast: An Invitation to the Christian Spiritual Life* by Marjorie J. Thompson. © 1995 by Marjorie J. Thompson. Used by permission.
[2] From *Soul Feast.*

Living Simply

Signs of the Spirit

Discuss where you have seen God's Spirit at work this week. How have you experienced grace in a new way through Christian practice? Discuss any joys or struggles you had. How is it with your soul?

Purpose

Because we long for Christ to be formed in us, we make this covenant to tend the fires of our souls so that our longing for Christ may never be extinguished and that our lives will be set ablaze with his love.

> Strive first for the kingdom of God and his righteousness, and all these things will be given to you as well.
> —Matthew 6:33

Instruction

Do you overbook your days chasing here, there, and everywhere? Have you ever had to collect your scattered self so you could make an important decision? Do you let the stuff you own lead your life? ever lay awake at night thinking about all you have to do? ever think about why your life is so full? ever wonder if it makes any difference at all? If this is you, simplicity must sound like an oasis in the desert of your frantic life.

But simplicity isn't a pill that promises to cure burnout and fatigue. It doesn't come from typing your schedule into a whiz-bang techno-organizer. It isn't a planner or a new way to multi-task. Living simply is not about deciding to get your life under control but about giving control of your life to God.

On the Inside

Talk as a group about all that controls your life. What do you treasure? Who owns you? to what are you attached? What part of your life takes up most of your energy? What do you do because of who you know? What do you do because of what you own?

Jesus talks about our wealth and our worries (Matthew 6:19-33). His bottom line is about as simple as simplicity gets: seek God, trust God, and receive God. With a partner, determine how far you are from living simply.

Soul-Tending: Life-Forming Practices for Older Youth & Young Adults

- How much of a turn will it take to clear the way and get your life pointed toward God?

- How close are you to trading worry for trust? to believing that God will take care of your basic needs? to receiving all God supplies as a gift?

Outward Reality

Imagine that you and your friends meet to eat, and no one comes to the table empty-handed. Everyone comes with a backpack or briefcase full of the stuff of their lives. If you unpacked them and put all the stuff on the table, what would you see?

Simplicity means clearing away the clutter (on the inside and outside, modifying your feelings about wealth, and changing the way you calculate your worth).

For a few minutes, play a "what if?" game. What if you left some of your important stuff on the table? What if you walked away from the table, taking only what is necessary for you to live? What would the things left on the table say to your friends about you?

Take a few moments alone to reflect on these questions:

> Gain all you can.
>
> Save all you can.
>
> Give all you can.
>
> —John Wesley[1]

- What does living simply have to do with your spiritual life and your relationship with God?

- What does the source of your power and wealth (Deuteronomy 8:17-19) have to do with your faith?

- How might you live simply in our consumer culture?

Living simply is centered on the desire to seek and know God. Its outside-in/inside-out complexities clearly point to a great gospel "absurdity": losing your life to find it (Matthew 16:25-26). Losing the stuff of your life to make room for God really saves your life.

 # Rehearsal

Take turns making a list of all the stuff you usually carry around in your backpack or purse. If you have it with you, dump it out. Choose to lose one thing that represents your own efforts and riches. What will you leave behind? What difference might your choice make in your relationship with God?

As a group, make a top ten list of clutter you want to clear from your lives. Brainstorm some strategies for loosening its grip on your life.

Draw a rough sketch of your favorite living space on a piece of paper. Look around for "luxuries." Put an *X* through any luxury that has become a necessity for you. Share your X's with the rest of your group. Talk together about how to really "X" these things from your lives.

nvolving

What kind of ripples might (or have) come about from living simply? How could your daily routine change by the transformation taking place in your soul? Discuss how you might see all areas of your life—home, school, nature, community, world, job, paying bills, and so forth—connected in a new way based on your spiritual formation journey.

omorrow

❑ Living simply is centered on the desire to seek and know God. See how much time in a day you are really seeking God and are aware of God's presence.

❑ Practice planned spending. Make a budget and stick to it. Pay cash when you shop.

❑ Part of living simply is understanding that God's provisions are gifts—not ours to keep. Our ancestors freed God's gifts during the year of Jubilee (Leviticus 25:8-55). Celebrate a day of Jubilee by freely sharing your God-given riches with others.

❑ Simplicity is an outward sign of an inward grace. Nurture this spiritual practice by integrating it with other spiritual disciplines. Try fasting as a way to see what owns and controls your life (see pages 57–60).

❑ Go to the Alternatives for Simple Living website at *www.simpleliving.org* to find other practical ideas for simplifying your life.

Notes
[1] Adapted from Wesley's Sermon, "On the Danger of Increasing Riches." Wesley preached that doing these things would "extract the poison from riches."

Solitude

 **igns of the Spirit**

Discuss where you have seen God's Spirit at work this week. How have you experienced grace in a new way through Christian practice? Discuss any joys or struggles you had. How is it with your soul?

 **urpose**

Because we long for Christ to be formed in us, we make this covenant to tend the fires of our souls so that our longing for Christ may never be extinguished and that our lives will be set ablaze with his love.

 **nstruction**

On My Own

In your mind, review a typical day in your life. With whom do you interact? Are there any times when you are alone? How would you measure the balance of time spent alone or with others? Can you estimate a percentage? Would you prefer more time by yourself or more time with other people?

Jesus Sought Solitude

Before Jesus began his ministry, he spent forty days alone in the desert (Matthew 4:1-11). He again spent time alone before choosing his disciples (Luke 6:12). In Matthew 14:13, we read that when he heard of the death of John the Baptist Jesus "withdrew from there in a boat to a deserted place by himself." In his short ministry, Jesus was constantly surrounded by people who wanted him to preach, teach, heal, and change their lives. As a counterbalance to this sometimes frenzied activity, Jesus consistently went away to be alone.

❖ What do you think Jesus did while he was alone?

❖ How did this time apart strengthen his ministry?

Alone Is Not Lonely

Jesus and many others over the centuries have found that solitude is a necessary ingredient of a healthy spiritual life. To practice solitude is to designate time with God only. Prayer, journaling, and reading Scripture are all ways to spend quiet time with God. Some people go on silent retreats for days at a time. Others have a focused quiet time every day where they meet God in the solitude. What about busy people who live constantly around other people? How can they make time for solitude?

If you're a person who likes to lie in bed for a few minutes after you awake but before you get up to start your day, you could designate this as "God time." Take a moment to talk to God and hear what God might say to you. Similarly, if it takes you time to fall asleep at night, let that be a solitude with God. If you run or work out by yourself, dedicate that alone time with God. Find ways to build solitude into your already existing routine, even if it means staying an extra fifteen minutes in the bathroom to brush your teeth!

Just Be With God

A healthy spiritual life includes extended times set apart to be alone with God. Perhaps you are often the only one at home on Wednesday evenings. You might keep a weekly "appointment" with God in prayer, Bible study, journaling, or whatever helps you connect to God. On a nice day you could go alone to a park or the library—any place where you would feel comfortable sitting in silence with God.

> Settle yourself in solitude and you will come upon Him in yourself.
> —Teresa of Avila

 ehearsal

❖ Finish the following sentences and discuss your answers:
I like to be alone when _____.
The hardest thing about being alone is _____.
To me, solitude means _____.
The difference between being alone and being in solitude
is _____.

❖ Read Mark 6:30-32. Why do you think Jesus said this to his disciples? Have there been times in your lives when you benefited from resting awhile or wished you had been able to go somewhere by yourself to do so?

❖ Many Native American tribes have a tradition of "vision quest" for young people, a time apart where a young person is alone in nature to ask for vision for the future. How might you adapt vision quest for your own spiritual journey?

Soul-Tending: Life-Forming Practices for Older Youth & Young Adults

 nvolving

What kind of ripples might (or have) come about from practicing solitude? How could your daily routine change by the transformation taking place in your soul? Discuss how you might see all areas of your life—home, school, nature, community, world, job, paying bills, and so forth—connected in a new way based on your spiritual formation journey.

 omorrow

❑ Make time to be alone with God. You could think about any of these questions, and/or write in your journal, and/or pray: Where have I recently seen God? For what am I thankful? Is there any problem I need to turn over to God?

❑ Take time in solitude to read Scripture. Try reading slowly, stopping to think about what you are reading. Some good places to start: Psalm 139; 1 Corinthians 13:1-13; Philippians 2:1-11; and 1 John 4:7-21.

❑ Talk to your parents or friends about what you've learned about solitude. Ask if they feel a need for more alone time. How can you support each other to meet those needs?

❑ Research some of the "spiritual giants" to see how they incorporated solitude into their lives. Go online to learn about Teresa de Avila, Saint Francis of Assisi, Hildegarde of Bingen, Martin Luther King, Jr., Henri Nouwen, Catherine De Hueck Doherty, and Carlo Carretto.

❑ Commit yourself to ten minutes alone with God each day.

❑ Listen for the times when you hear God's nudging to go and be away from other people. As you begin to attune your life to God's nudges, you will find that seeking quiet alone time becomes second nature.

Testimony

Signs of the Spirit

Discuss where you have seen God's Spirit at work this week. How have you experienced grace in a new way through Christian practice? Discuss any joys or struggles you had. How is it with your soul?

Purpose

Because we long for Christ to be formed in us, we make this covenant to tend the fires of our souls so that our longing for Christ may never be extinguished and that our lives will be set ablaze with his love.

Instruction

Jesus mostly taught by storytelling and by his actions. We know how we are to love others because of the real-life examples he gave us through story and by the way he reached out to love all people, even those on the fringes. But there is one message that Jesus gave to us plainly and simply: Go and tell others about him. This practice is sometimes referred to as "testimony"— the sharing of our Christian experience. We learn by exploring the Scriptures that testimonies can be very different.

Discuss the differences and similarities in these testimonies:

> You will be my witnesses in Jerusalem, in Judea and Samaria, and to the ends of the earth.
> —Acts 1:8

❖ Paul retells (Acts 22:6-16; 26:12-18) his Damascus Road experience (Acts 9) in which he is blinded but given true sight by Christ.

❖ Two disciples tell the story of unknowingly walking with Jesus and only knowing it was him when he broke bread (Luke 24:33-35).

❖ Paul, writing to Timothy, recalls the faith of Timothy's grandmother, Lois, and his mother Eunice, and now recognizes that same faith in Timothy (2 Timothy 1).

Soul-Tending: Life-Forming Practices for Older Youth & Young Adults

Our life stories and faith experiences are all different, yet it is the same Lord who meets us in those different places. Sometimes we are drawn to almost unbelievable testimonies when the good news of Christ seems too good to be true! Testimonies of less spectacular events are generally more believable to us, yet we tend to question the importance of these events in shaping our testimonies.

❖ In your own life, what events, people, and/or places shape your testimony? Discuss and write any thoughts below.

Beverly Burton is a professional storyteller. Her experiences growing up in a rural community left her with many memories that she often shares in her stories. Her stories describe a particular place and the people who lived there. Surrounded by grandparents, aunts, uncles, and cousins, Beverly can relate to Timothy. Recalling memories of events that involved some of these relatives, she tells stories that teach lessons of respect, responsibility, and love. Initially when telling these stories, Beverly didn't refer to them as her testimony. But after reflecting on the way they have molded her faith, she began to see them as part of her testimony. She is reminded of the faith of her grandmother and her mother, along with many others. In this way, she is able to recognize that same faith in her own life—just as Paul recognized Timothy's faith!

> This is my story,
> this is my song,
> praising my Savior
> all the day long.
> —Fanny Crosby,
> "Blessed Assurance"

Have someone read aloud the lyric from "Blessed Assurance." Do you have stories from your own life that you have never thought of as being part of your testimony? Reflect on these stories, people, and places. Consider how much they have shaped your personal testimony—your relationship with Jesus Christ. What is your story and song?

The Bible can be understood as a book that contains the testimonies of the spiritual giants that have gone before us.

❖ Read or recall the experiences of Isaiah, Miriam, Peter, or Mary. How might you sense the wonderful way in which God meets us in our everyday lives?

God's grace has such an effect on us that we must tell our story—and it is good news. Discuss the following questions:

❖ What is your testimony?

❖ What does your life tell about your faith?

 ehearsal

In this session and in every session through the practice of identifying with one another the "signs of the Spirit" at the beginning of each session, you are gaining experience in giving testimony to God's presence in your life. Discuss any new insights you might have about your story.

Our testimonies are not something we keep to ourselves. We have a great, great story to tell. Discuss these questions as you consider how you might live in such a way that others will come to know that story:

❖ What prevents you from sharing your faith or giving a testimony?
❖ What has been most unique about your faith experiences in your life so far?
❖ What are some ways other than verbally a testimony might be shared?

 nvolving

What kind of ripples might (or have) come about from knowing and sharing your testimony? How could your daily routine change by the transformation taking place in your soul? Discuss how you might see all areas of your life—home, school, nature, community, world, job, paying bills, and so forth—connected in a new way based on your spiritual formation journey.

 omorrow

❏ Begin to write your faith story this week. Start with, "A time in my life when I felt close to God was _____" and add to it each day.

❏ Ask one of your parents to tell you about his or her own faith.

❏ Write a letter or email to someone who has shaped your Christian faith. Express your gratitude for that person's testimony, telling him or her of its importance to you.

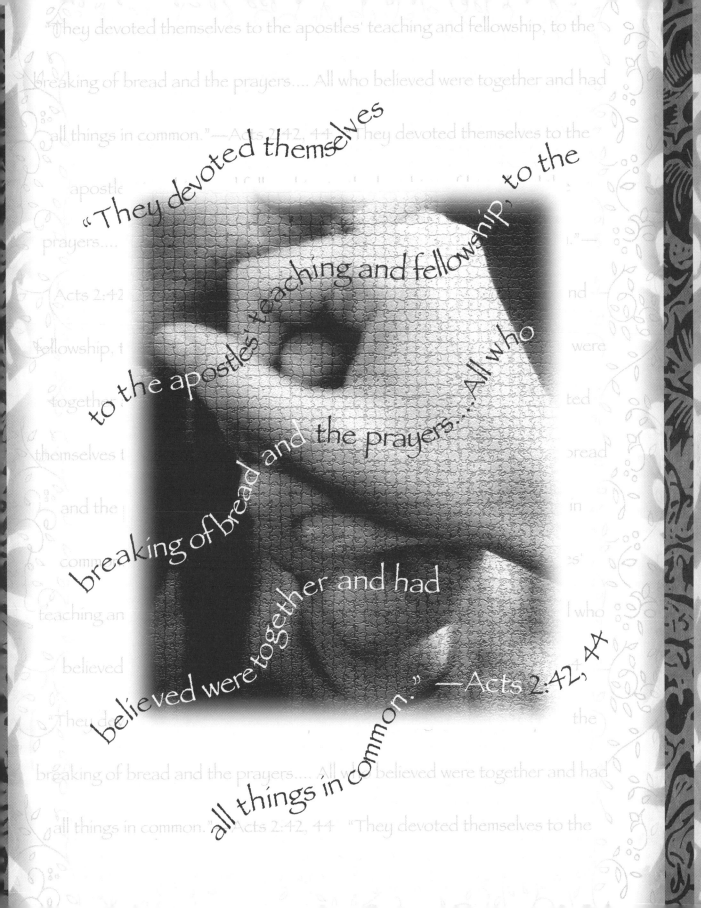

"They devoted themselves to the apostles' teaching and fellowship, to the breaking of bread and the prayers.... All who believed were together and had all things in common." —Acts 2:42, 44

I used to love singing in the choir at church. I would rush home from school every Wednesday to get to church early for rehearsal. Our director had incredible energy and loved kids, so I loved being there. From the time I was five, I was singing solos in church. That's why I couldn't understand why I got passed up for the lead in the Christmas musical when I was twelve. I was crushed. I thought Mrs. Mitchell no longer liked me, and I went home that afternoon vowing never to return.

The next week when I didn't show up for rehearsal, Mrs. Mitchell came by the house. In a very gentle and loving way, she explained to an angry and hurt pre-teen that God did not intend for twelve-year-old boys to sing alone. I was needed for other reasons, and I would add more to the pageant than just my voice.

> The journey of faith is never intended to be a solo act.

In the same way, God did not intend for Christians to "sing alone." Paul uses the image of a human body. Imagine an ear cutting itself off from the body and trying to live apart from it—the picture is ridiculous. According to Paul, we are all gifted in different ways that create a whole body. For the same reason that we do not see ears bouncing around on our streets, our spiritual life cannot be separated from the body of Christ.

Sometimes we might trick ourselves into believing that our faith is strictly a personal matter and that we can go it alone. But Christ calls us to live a life of faith in which we are a part of the communion (body) of Christ.

The spiritual practices that we do in a community of other Christians help to mold us in the image of Christ. These practices help us to "tend together" the fire of our souls so that we can, as a communion of Christ's body, give light and heat to a hurting world. When we unite together as a communion of believers, we become part of one another's stories. "If one part suffers, every part suffers with it; if one part is honored, every part rejoices with it" (1 Corinthians 12:26, NIV). The depth of this Scripture is often glossed over as a sentimental suggestion for a community. However, as a communion of Christ's body, our lives truly become part of a common story. We have a covenantal responsibility to bear one another's burdens, share one another's sorrows, and celebrate one another's joy.

"Tending together" requires a stern commitment to covenant and accountability. The people who join with us on our journey long for Christ to be formed in us. That means being accountable to them for our spiritual growth and helping to hold them accountable for theirs.

The journey of faith is never intended to be a solo act. Like a pre-adolescent boy attempting to sing a solo, our efforts to "go it alone" can be damaging to ourselves and others. However, when we are in communion with other Christians and share a commitment to spiritual formation, God will take our individual voices and blend them into a beautiful harmony singing God's praise.

Sacraments

 **igns of the Spirit**

Discuss where you have seen God's Spirit at work this week. How have you experienced grace in a new way through Christian practice? Discuss any joys or struggles you had. How is it with your soul?

 **urpose**

Because we long for Christ to be formed in us, we make this covenant to tend the fires of our souls so that our longing for Christ may never be extinguished and that our lives will be set ablaze with his love.

> One does not understand a mystery, one experiences it.
> —James F. White,
> *Sacraments as God's Self Giving*[1]

 **nstruction**

It happened the same way every time. Just after I acknowledged the judge and just before I started my routine, I would find my mom in the crowd to see her smile and give me the thumbs up. This ritual during every gymnastics meet was not extraordinary because it made my routines perfect or because it took away all my fears. The extraordinary thing was that my mom smiled and gave me the thumbs up no matter what the state of our relationship was. Proud, annoyed, excited, or angry, my mom always looked directly into my eyes and gave me the thumbs up.

❖ Is there someone in your life who has faith in you no matter what?

❖ How has that person's actions expressed his or her love and confidence in you?

Ordinary Made Extraordinary

Sacraments are simply the ordinary things we do through which God gives extraordinary grace. Through baptism, God conveys grace to allow us to begin our lives anew. Through Holy Communion, God conveys saving grace and power over death in Christ. Thankfully the sacraments are not dependent on our faithfulness as a people or our worthiness as individuals. Baptism and Holy Communion are God's gifts to us—God's beloved children.

The consistency of unconditional love from my mom helps me understand the sacraments. God does not withhold the sacrament of baptism because there are hungry children in the world. Instead God continues to work in people's hearts bringing children to baptism to remind us through the sacrament that all children are God's children worthy of love, safety, and care. Similarly, God does not deny anyone Communion until he or she is worthy but invites us to the table.

We find God waiting for each of us as we celebrate Holy Communion, ready to reveal again God's power over death by forgiving our sins and showering us with grace. The sacraments are not merely memorized words to help us imagine events in the distant past but new and real experiences of God. The sacraments are tactile ways of experiencing God. We feel the water and taste the bread and wine. In these seemingly ordinary acts, God is present in the most extraordinary way.

❖ How are baptism and Communion celebrated in your church?

❖ Is everyone made to feel welcome? How?

❖ Does the service itself help you to understand the sacraments as God's gift to you? How?

> The vertical relationship to Christ is matched by horizontal union to each other.
> —James F. White, *Sacraments as God's Self Giving*[2]

Baptism

Through baptism we are adopted into the family of God and brought into the covenant God made in Jesus Christ. The church promises to nurture and love us as we grow in faith. If you remember your baptism, tell about your experience. If you were baptized as an infant, tell about what you imagine it to have been like or what your parents told you about it.

When we are baptized, we are forever sealed into God's love. Sometimes, though, we may feel we need to renew our baptismal covenant. Have you ever participated in a baptismal renewal service? What was it like?

Holy Communion

The sacrament of Holy Communion is the covenant family meal. By taking Communion, we participate in an ancient act that physically connects us to God. What are your feelings about Holy Communion? What are some of your most meaningful experiences of taking Communion?

The Sacraments and Our Faith Walk

Read the quotation by James F. White. Through baptism and Communion, a community is bound together by God's forgiveness and a vision of the kingdom of God where equality, unity, and justice will reign with love. Coming together on Sunday mornings to baptize or break bread together is not to gain personal access to salvation or to recharge our individual spiritual batteries. This time together is to remember we are God's children called as Jesus was to spread the gospel and seek peace in our world.

The sacraments are also one of the few times in our lives when we receive without having to give something in return. The sacraments are not about what we have done but about what God can and is doing for us. God has claimed us as

Soul-Tending: Life-Forming Practices for Older Youth & Young Adults

God's own in baptism, pouring out the Holy Spirit that will continue to call us, meet us, and empower us as we receive Communion.

❖ How might participating in the sacraments nurture your soul and strengthen your community of faith?

 ehearsal

Using your church's book of worship, have a renewal of baptism service. Also, invite your pastor to bless and serve Communion for your group.

 nvolving

What kind of ripples might (or have) come about from practicing the sacraments regularly? How could your daily routine change by the transformation taking place in your soul? Discuss how you might see all areas of your life—home, school, nature, community, world, job, paying bills, and so forth—connected in a new way based on your spiritual formation journey.

 omorrow

❑ Read the ritual of baptism for your church. How have your parents and congregation lived up to those promises in your life? How have you lived out the promises you have made during each baptism service you have participated in? How would your church and the world look different if those promises were always faithfully kept?

❑ At a Communion service, pay special attention to the taste, smell, and texture of the bread and wine. Look for God present in this moment. Journal about your impressions.

Notes

[1] Reprinted from *Sacraments as God's Self Giving*, by James F. White, copyright © 1983 by Abingdon Press, page 66. All rights reserved. Used by permission.
[2] From *Sacraments as God's Self Giving*, page 38.

Common Worship

igns of the Spirit

Discuss where you have seen God's Spirit at work this week. How have you experienced grace in a new way through Christian practice? Discuss any joys or struggles you had. How is it with your soul?

urpose

Because we long for Christ to be formed in us, we make this covenant to tend the fires of our souls so that our longing for Christ may never be extinguished and that our lives will be set ablaze with his love.

nstruction

Discuss the following questions:

❖ How many years have you been attending a church?
❖ How many different places have you worshiped? What was a favorite one?
❖ Why do you attend worship services (or why don't you attend worship services)?
❖ What is a highlight in worship for you personally?
❖ What is a lowlight in worship for you personally?

> I think that worship, even a very traditional form of worship can become more meaningful if we're willing to prepare ourselves. . . . And if I do that, I will bring something to the worship, and I will begin hearing little echoes and resonances and things that I wouldn't have heard if I hadn't prepared myself.
>
> —Marjorie Thompson[1]

Why Worship?

Worship is the gathering of God's people to praise, honor, and glorify God. Common worship is vital to our life of faith. First of all, common worship reminds us that we aren't lone rangers in our faith. We cannot be Christians in isolation, for it is only together that we are the body of Christ. You may find that worship is sometimes uncomfortable because you find yourself surrounded not only by the friends you love but also by hypocrites, by people who irritate you, by those who don't approve of what you are wearing, by toddlers who are noisy and disruptive, and by others whom you just plain don't like. And this motley crew is the very body of Christ with whom we are called to worship and serve. If we worship only with people our own age or only with people we really like, we miss out on the amazing grace of a God who brings us together as a community of forgiven sinners. Worship teaches us that we are made for communion not only with God but also with one another.

We gather in worship to remember who we are and whose we are. In worship, we hear the stories of our family of faith—stories of God's love and God's people that have been passed down through the ages. This "proclamation" part of worship is like listening to your grandmother tell stories about your dad when he was young. In listening, you find out more about who you are. In worship, we are nurtured as a family of faith through the sacraments. These visible signs of God's grace claim us as children of God and strengthen us for Christ's service. In public worship, we hear the stories of God's grace, and we give thanks for God's love that will never let us go. In her book, *Amazing Grace*, Kathleen Norris talks about worship as a response to grace and a celebration for God's continued faith in us—God's children.

The Theatre of Worship

Have one person in your group be the director. Designate one person to be God and one person to represent the minister. The rest of the group is the congregation. Have the director arrange God, the congregation, and the minister to describe the way he or she thinks worship happens. For instance, is God in the middle of the crowd or off in the distance? Is the congregation asleep? Is God asleep? Is the minister talking too much?

> So when you leave worship, the question to ask isn't "How was it?" but "How did I do?"

After the director has arranged worship, have him or her explain what he or she did and why. Then select a new director and start over. The last director can arrange the group to fit Kierkegaard's metaphor of the theatre of worship. Soren Kierkegaard was a Danish Christian philosopher who lived during the 1800's. He said that worship is like a play. Many of us imagine that the ministers are the actors in the play and that the congregation is the audience. The truth is that the congregation members are the actors with the minister and the choir coaching them to do their best for the audience—God. So, when you leave worship, the question to ask isn't "How was it?" but "How did I do?"

❖ What new insights have you gained through this exercise?

Hold on to Your Seats

We gather in worship to praise God, but God also uses worship to transform us. Through the music, the preaching, the prayers, and especially through the sacraments, God is powerfully at work in our lives. The Holy Spirit sometimes grabs hold of us in worship and "moves" us to a new place.

❖ Has worship ever "moved" you to tears? to praise? to peace? to a new way of life?

Take a few minutes to think about an experience of common worship that had a powerful impact on you. Close your eyes and try to remember the experience and how it moved you. After a few minutes, turn to a neighbor and tell about your experience. Write any insights below.

Boring!

Let's face it. Worship doesn't always move us. Worship, especially Sunday morning traditional worship, can be boring and frustrating. We know God is with us when we gather for worship, but sometimes it feels like God is yawning, too. In many churches, worship is designed for and by adults, with little thought given to how the service might be relevant for younger members of the body of Christ.

Discuss the following:

❖ So how do we faithfully engage in the practice of common worship with an attitude of praise and thanksgiving, rather than one of simply duty and obligation?

Get Involved

Add your voice to those of the adults who discuss and plan worship in your congregation. Discuss the following questions:

❖ What do you think is the most important part of the worship service for adults in your church?
❖ What is the most important part for younger persons?
❖ If you and your friends could change some things in worship, what would they be, and how do you think others in the congregation would react?

Preparing Our Hearts

The other way we can faithfully engage in worship that we find boring is to prepare our own hearts. We can prepare for worship through prayer. We can pray for the worship leaders. We can pray that God will meet us in worship and speak a personal word to us. We can pray for our hearts to be open to the movement of the Holy Spirit.

We can prepare for worship by spending time with the Scripture text. If your pastor preaches from the lectionary, you know in advance what the texts will be, and you can spend time reflecting on or even discussing them with some friends.

We can prepare for worship as we engage in other spiritual disciplines. As we weave Scripture reading, prayer, acts of hospitality, and bearing witness into our daily lives, we will find our minds and hearts open to receive God's grace. As we prepare, we can be confident that God will be with us in common worship and that we will be made one with the body of Christ, the church.

 ehearsal

Join your hearts in a time of worship. Use a liturgy for a service of evening prayer from your denominational book of worship or the *Book of Common Prayer*. Afterward, debrief the experience.

❖ How did you do?

 nvolving

What kind of ripples might (or have) come about from practicing common worship? How could your daily routine change by the transformation taking place in your soul? Discuss how you might see all areas of your life—home, school, nature, community, world, job, paying bills, and so forth—connected in a new way based on your spiritual formation journey.

 omorrow

❑ Prepare for worship by praying each day this week for the worship leaders and that your own heart would be open to God's leading.

❑ Call your pastor to find out the sermon text for this week's worship service. Prepare for worship by meditating on the Scripture passages each day.

❑ Set up a meeting with others interested in worship in your youth group, campus group, or congregation to discuss how you might be more actively engaged in worship.

❑ Volunteer to read Scripture or lead a prayer in a worship service at your church.

Notes
[1] *Cloud of Witnesses: An Audio Journal on Youth, Church, and Culture; Volume Two, Spirituality* (Princeton Theological Institute for Youth Ministry, Copyright © 2001), Track 8.

Catechesis and Confirmation

igns of the Spirit

Discuss where you have seen God's Spirit at work this week. How have you experienced grace in a new way through Christian practice? Discuss any joys or struggles you had. How is it with your soul?

urpose

Because we long for Christ to be formed in us, we make this covenant to tend the fires of our souls so that our longing for Christ may never be extinguished and that our lives will be set ablaze with his love.

nstruction

As baptized members of the church, we are already part of the family of God. Through confirmation, we respond publicly to the promise of baptism, pledging to obey and follow Christ. In confirmation, we say what we believe, telling the church and the world that we profess Jesus Christ as Lord and Savior. Confirmation is like beginning a journey. It is a first step in becoming who we are in Christ. As baptized members of the church, we are already Christians and part of the family of God. Confirmation publicly marks your intention to be who God created you to be and to follow Christ all the days of your life. Discuss your feelings or questions about confirmation.

Getting to Confirmation

To be confirmed, you participate in a confirmation class or catechesis depending on your denomination. Confirmation class and catechesis are two ways of learning the history of our faith. Confirmation class is an in-depth exploration of the history of the church, doctrine, social principles, and the covenant story. Catechism teaches the same information through memorization of questions and responses. Both lead up to a confirmation service in which you confirm your faith in God by proclaiming the Apostles' Creed as your statement of belief.

Adopting a Mission Statement

By being confirmed, you adopt the mission statement of the church: the Apostles' Creed. You stand before the congregation and say the Apostles' Creed together with the congregation. You might think this act is not a big deal—just some old words that we don't understand or a nice tradition in the church. But it is a very big deal. When you accept the promises that God has made to you, you are claiming God's promises for yourself. You belong to a God who loves you enough to die for you. God has given you a new identity and the strength and courage to live out that identity. God has called you to live not as a lone ranger, but in community—to live and work and laugh and serve with others. When you accept these promises and respond to them by standing before the church and the world and reciting the Apostles' Creed as your own mission statement, your life will never be the same.

Know What You Are Getting Into

As you prepare to be confirmed, you have a special responsibility to learn the basics of the Christian faith. The point is not for you to memorize a bunch of information and pass a test. Rather, catechetical instruction is intended to help you realize what is at stake in standing before the church and confessing your faith in Jesus Christ as your Lord and Savior. This decision is not to be taken lightly, and you should be fully informed. Confirming your faith is a commitment that will change the course of your life in ways that you cannot now imagine. Studying the amazing story of faith is an opportunity to learn about the big picture of Christian faith and to ask plenty of questions about what it means to be a Christian.

A Language of Faith

As you are confirmed and grow in your Christian faith, you learn a new language. Getting involved in a new activity often involves learning new terminology. If you want to play the oboe, you need to learn to read music. It's hard to excel in basketball if you don't know what a foul is. If you were moving to Paris, you would want to learn to speak French. So it is with being a Christian. The Christian language helps us to experience and live out our faith. Catechisms and confirmation classes help us to learn that new language.

Discuss the following questions and write any thoughts below:

❖ If you have been confirmed in the church, what do you remember about that day? Did you understand what you were doing? How has it affected the way in which you live now?

❖ If you have not yet been confirmed in the church, what has kept you from making that declaration of faith?

❖ What is the importance of catechesis and confirmation in the life of faith?

Studying and Learning as a Spiritual Discipline

Catechisms and confirmation classes aren't just for education. Meditating and reflecting on these truths of our faith deepen our experience of God and provide a bedrock of trust in difficult times. As you go through your life, you will find that lessons you learned preparing for confirmation become lived out in the world around you. Discuss these questions and write any thoughts below.

❖ What did you learn about God through catechesis or confirmation class that has become real to you now?

❖ How might remembering the catechisms and renewing our confirmation of faith tend the fires of our souls?

 ehearsal

Read the Apostles' Creed aloud together. Discuss your thoughts after having read it together.

❖ What does it mean to you to proclaim these words?

The Apostles' Creed, Ecumenical Version

I believe in God, the Father Almighty, creator of heaven and earth.

I believe in Jesus Christ, his only Son, our Lord, who was conceived by the Holy Spirit, born of the Virgin Mary, suffered under Pontius Pilate, was crucified, died, and was buried; he descended to the dead. On the third day he rose again; he ascended into heaven, is seated at the right hand of the Father, and will come again to judge the living and the dead.

I believe in the Holy Spirit, the holy catholic church, the communion of saints, the forgiveness of sins, the resurrection of the body, and the life everlasting. Amen.

❖ In what ways does this proclamation lead you in living a holy life?

 nvolving

What kind of ripples might (or have) come about from practicing confirmation and catechesis? How could your daily routine change by the transformation taking place in your soul? Discuss how you might see all areas of your life—home, school, nature, community, world, job, paying bills, and so forth—connected in a new way based on your spiritual formation journey.

 omorrow

❑ If you haven't yet been confirmed, plan a time to talk with your pastor, campus minister, or youth leader about what is involved and what steps you need to take to be confirmed.

❑ If you have been confirmed, keep a journal this week about ways your profession of faith in Christ makes a difference in your life.

❑ Choose a question and answer of the catechism to meditate on for the week. Read it each night before you go to bed and when you wake up in the morning. Look for connections between the question and answer you chose and the world around you. Write about these connections in a journal.

❑ Write your own catechism question and answer. What is a question you have about faith? Do some research and talk with some trusted mentors to find an answer.

❑ Memorize the Apostles' Creed and say it every morning when you wake up as a declaration before you go about your day.

❑ Read the confirmation service in your book of worship.

Christian Fellowship

 **igns of the Spirit**

Discuss where you have seen God's Spirit at work this week. How have you experienced grace in a new way through Christian practice? Discuss any joys or struggles you had. How is it with your soul?

 **urpose**

Because we long for Christ to be formed in us, we make this covenant to tend the fires of our souls so that our longing for Christ may never be extinguished and that our lives will be set ablaze with his love.

> If Thy heart be as my heart,
> give me Thy hand.
> —John Wesley

 **nstruction**

Connected Through Christ

Whenever Christians gather, they do so in the name of Jesus. He is the hidden guest at every congregational meeting, potluck dinner, church softball game, or youth lock-in. Read the following passages to help you discuss the questions below: Acts 2:43-47; Ephesians 4:1-6; and 1 John 4:7-21.

❖ What makes a group of Christians unlike any other group of people?

❖ How is the focus of your youth group or campus fellowship different from a school club, sports team, student council, or fraternity or sorority?

Woven Together as One

Sit in a circle. Take a ball of yarn and tie one end to someone's wrist. That person should name someone in the group who has been personally supportive of him or her, then throw the ball of yarn to that person. Each participant repeats this process, carefully holding on to the piece of yarn as the ball is thrown, until everyone in the circle has held the yarn at least once. Take a moment to look at the way the yarn threads its way around the circle, linking everyone together. Read these words from Colossians 3:14: "Love is more important than anything else. It is what ties everything completely together" (CEV).

Find God, Share God, or Both?

In Alice Walker's book, *The Color Purple*, Shug talks about going to church to share God as opposed to finding God in church. Discuss:

❖ Do people find God in church, do they bring God with them, or both?

❖ How is it possible to share a spiritual experience (for instance, in a worship service) when those gathered don't necessarily know one another?

❖ What is it that binds Christians together?

Growing Together in Love

Every church congregation, fellowship group, or Christian youth organization has its own personality, but there are certain things they hold in common. Brainstorm a list of what goals such groups might have.

Then have someone read Colossians 3:12-17 as if this were a job description for your group. Discuss opinions on how well your group does at these various tasks. Be specific, as in "I like it when we sing together but I don't think we are a very patient group," or "Even though we are not all best friends, I feel loved and accepted here." What might you want to change about your group that would help you act out your faith as Paul encouraged the church at Colossae to act?

Why Do We Need Each Other?

The image of a fire is often used in describing our need for Christian community: Coals burn longer when they are heaped in a fire with other coals. When one is separated and no longer shares the warmth of the fire, it will become cold. How is this a helpful image for Christians? What other images come to mind? Think together about the many reasons why Christian fellowship is important.

Fellowship Is a Choice

Christian fellowship helps us on our spiritual journey because in it we find persons who have a genuine desire to help us grow and from whom we learn about our faith. We cannot be faithful followers of Jesus Christ in isolation. Jesus surrounded himself with others who would be a support system.

❖ In what ways have you grown spiritually through Christian fellowship?

ehearsal

Have someone read aloud the quotation from John Wesley. Wesley strongly believed that in Christian fellowship, God's grace was made known to us through simply fellowshipping with other believers. Enjoy a time of relaxed fellowship with one another. You may want to provide snacks. Read the quotation aloud again, this time in unison and join hands. Spend a moment in prayer thanking God for the fellowship of your small group.

nvolving

What kind of ripples might (or have) come about from practicing Christian fellowship? How could your daily routine change by the transformation taking place in your soul? Discuss how you might see all areas of your life—home, school, nature, community, world, job, paying bills, and so forth—connected in a new way based on your spiritual formation journey.

omorrow

❑ Take time each day this week to pray for members of your faith community.

❑ In your journal, write out the names of those persons who have supported you in your spiritual growth or shared their own faith journeys with you. Spend time in prayer each day this week thanking God for their fellowship with you.

❑ Do you think it is significant that the New Testament has numerous instances where we see Jesus eating with friends, relaxing with his disciples, and talking about faith with individuals? How would the New Testament story be different if Jesus had held himself apart from the community?

❑ Using any art form you enjoy, fashion a representation of how you see Christian fellowship.

Covenanting

igns of the Spirit

Discuss where you have seen God's Spirit at work this week. How have you experienced grace in a new way through Christian practice? Discuss any joys or struggles you had. How is it with your soul?

urpose

Because we long for Christ to be formed in us, we make this covenant to tend the fires of our souls so that our longing for Christ may never be extinguished and that our lives will be set ablaze with his love.

nstruction

How many commitments do you think you make in the course of one day—even beyond the daily, unavoidable commitments of work, internships, homework, helping out around the house, student council meetings, fraternity or sorority meetings, or practice after classes? How many people have you promised your time, effort, gifts, or service? You may have offered to give a friend a ride to school, lead devotions at youth group on Sunday, babysit for your little brother, or make dinner for your mom. Take a minute to think about your schedule and discuss the kinds of commitments you make in an average week.

❖ How easy is it to break commitments after you agreed to them?
❖ How important is keeping commitments in life?
❖ A commitment is an agreement that you make with someone or to something. What do you think is the meaning of the word *covenant*?

The scriptural meaning of *covenant* is to make a lasting agreement with God. Discuss how the following characteristics of covenanting are different from other agreements we make today like promises or contracts:

- ❖ Covenants are always centered in God.

- ❖ Covenants are never broken by God.

- ❖ Covenants are always permanent. They cannot be adjusted or amended, only broken.

Scripture tells the story of God's faithfulness in covenanting with us and our self-centeredness and idolatry. God remains faithful to the covenants made with Noah and with "all flesh that is on the earth" (Genesis 9:1-17), with Abraham, promising a multitude of descendants and land (Genesis 12:1-9), and renewed through Moses (Deuteronomy 5:1-21). Throughout the history of the Hebrew people, God's covenant was to be their God and not abandon them.

Even though the covenants were continually broken by imperfect and disobedient people, God offered a lasting and saving covenant through Jesus Christ. Obedience has always been the condition of the covenant relationship, and Christ's obedience brings us into that covenant with God. Our faith history teaches us that through baptism we are adopted into God's family and brought into covenant with God through Jesus Christ.

- ❖ What does it mean to you that God loves you so much that God would make a covenant with you to provide both salvation from sin and peace in life?

- ❖ God has promised to be our God. What is our responsibility in the covenant?

- ❖ In what other kinds of situations would a covenant be more appropriate than a simple contract or promise?

Covenants are made when God is the center of the agreement. Maybe you have made a covenant to one another in a small group and asked God to be the foundation on which the group holds together. Covenants are made in a marriage when God is the bond between two people. Our covenant with God means that we will give our lives to whatever God can use. We give up our selfish desires in covenants for the betterment of the relationship. We lay ourselves at God's feet for service, and we surrender our self-centeredness in relationships with others.

 ehearsal

In order to be faithful to our covenant with God we need the support and accountability of other believers. Read John 15:1-10. Discuss how the symbol of the vine and the branches helps you to understand the spiritual practice of covenanting.

 158

Consider these statements and discuss your thoughts:

❖ I have a difficult time living faithfully to my covenant with God because _____.

❖ Together as a group of disciples, we covenant to support and encourage one another by _____.

Close by praying together the covenant prayer.

 nvolving

What kind of ripples might (or have) come about from practicing covenanting? How could your daily routine change by the transformation taking place in your soul? Discuss how you might see all areas of your life—home, school, nature, community, world, job, paying bills, and so forth—connected in a new way based on your spiritual formation journey.

 omorrow

❑ Journal about a time or experience in the past when you were faithful. Was there a promise kept? Was it easy or difficult? Where was God in that experience?

❑ In what area of your life are you struggling to be faithful? Ask a friend to covenant with you to work on that area together.

❑ Read the story of Moses in Exodus. How was he faithful? What were the conditions of his covenant with God and with God's people? What enabled him to live out the covenant faithfully?

❑ What times have you been unfaithful? Spend some time in prayer asking God for forgiveness and thanking God for the grace and love to keep trying.

I am no longer my own, but thine. Put me to what thou wilt, rank me with whom thou wilt. Put me to doing, put me to suffering. Let me be employed by thee or laid aside for thee, exalted for thee or brought low by thee. Let me be full, let me be empty. Let me have all things, let me have nothing. I freely and heartily yield all things to thy pleasure and disposal. And now, O glorious and blessed God, Father, Son, and Holy Spirit, thou art mine, and I am thine. So be it. And the covenant which I have made on earth, let it be ratified in heaven.

Amen.

—A Covenant Prayer in the Wesleyan Tradition

Community Discernment

Signs of the Spirit

Discuss where you have seen God's Spirit at work this week. How have you experienced grace in a new way through Christian practice? Discuss any joys or struggles you had. How is it with your soul?

Purpose

Because we long for Christ to be formed in us, we make this covenant to tend the fires of our souls so that our longing for Christ may never be extinguished and that our lives will be set ablaze with his love.

Instruction

> Make me to know your ways, O LORD; teach me your paths.
> Lead me in your truth, and teach me, for you are the God of my salvation; for you I wait all day long.
> —Psalm 25:4-5

Rules or Discernment?

Decision-making is a part of daily life. Cereal or toast for breakfast? walk to school or catch a ride? finish the chemistry assignment today or wait until tomorrow? Not only do individuals have to work through large and small decisions, but groups are often called upon to make decisions together.

Most groups use the parliamentary system with Robert's Rules of Order as the final say. In this system, the people who are most familiar with Robert's Rules keep everyone else on track. A process with various procedures leads toward a firm decision at the end. Unfortunately, however, as helpful as this system can be, it does not always lead to a feeling of unity when a group votes on a given issue. Winners and losers are always a part of any vote that is not unanimous.

Seeing the Prism of Truth

More and more church groups use a process of discernment for decision-making where the goal is not only to make a decision but also to promote and maintain Christian unity. Group members take prayerful time together to consider the decision before them. The feeling of "If I can just out-talk people who hold different views, my side will win" does not exist in discernment. Instead, Danny Morris suggests placing the topic for discussion in the middle of the group where everyone can view it from a variety of perspectives. Morris compares the topic to a prism that casts light in different directions, depending on who is discussing it. After examination from a variety of people and their unique perspectives, the topic is turned in such a way so that it finally reflects the light of truth: God's will. In other words, talking and listening together in a prayerful spirit leads to the group's seeing the discussion topic in a new way. The process leads to a consensus, which is needed to bring clarity to the issue. Discuss what you see to be the main differences between using parliamentary procedure and discernment in group decision-making.

❖ What settings would benefit most from either process?

❖ What do you see as the pros and cons of using Robert's Rules of Order? of using discernment?

The Quadri-what?

Some decisions take all the resources we can muster. We may need to do research in a variety of areas before we have enough information to choose action A or action B. The Wesleyan tradition encourages the use of four sources as background for all our decision-making: Scripture, tradition, experience, and reason. We take our specific decision and first look to the Bible and the instruction we find on the issue. Then we add the tradition of our Judeo-Christian heritage: How has the church historically dealt with similar questions or situations? We apply what we have found to our own experience, then use our own reason to make the decision. This approach is called using the "Wesleyan Quadrilateral" (four-pronged method of decision-making).

❖ How does the Quadrilateral work in decision-making?

❖ What decisions does your group face? Discuss what methods of discernment you might use in making these decisions.

❖ The ultimate goal of decision-making is to further us down the path to holiness and life. What choices might move a person or group toward life? What choices might have the opposite effect?

❖ Read Acts 1:21-26 in which the early believers choose someone to take the place of Judas (who committed suicide after betraying Jesus). Compare this way of making a decision to what happened in Matthew 27:15-23.

❖ Discuss why some people think it is easier to use parliamentary procedure than to take the time for discernment. What sorts of decisions are more suited for discernment? for parliamentary procedure?

 ehearsal

Think of a real-life decision your group or church is in the process of making or might need to make in the future. State the topic clearly, then go through this process:

❖ What Scripture passages might inform our thinking on this issue? (You can use a concordance if you're not sure where to look.) Is everything in the Bible in agreement on this issue, or can you find conflicting ideas?

❖ Looking at the history of the church, can you find any practices or decisions (from church councils or writings) that inform your topic?

❖ Have each group member tell from personal experience a real-life story of how individuals might be affected by a decision one way or the other.

❖ With all this information, as a group apply your own reason or thinking processes. Look at Scripture, tradition, and experience as you make a decision that will affect your group as a whole, individuals, or even the life of the whole church.

 nvolving

What kind of ripples might (or have) come about from practicing community discernment? How could your daily routine change by the transformation taking place in your soul? Discuss how you might see all areas of your life—home, school, nature, community, world, job, paying bills, and so forth—connected in a new way based on your spiritual formation journey.

Tomorrow

☐ If you are facing a big decision, begin the process of discernment with your community of faith.

☐ Consider how you might be helpful to others who are wrestling with decision-making. Pray for them each day this week as they make their decision.

☐ Journal about a time when you solicited the help of a group in order to discern a decision or about a time you wished you had received such support.

☐ Research Quaker John Woolman and how the Society of Friends was able, through discernment and consensus, to voluntarily free their slaves more than one hundred years before the Civil War.

☐ Attend a meeting of one of the decision-making bodies at your church to see how they work through decisions.

☐ Read 1 Kings 3:5-14 each day this week. What would you say was King Solomon's attitude toward decision-making? What was God's response to Solomon?

Confession and Forgiveness in Community

 **igns of the Spirit**

Discuss where you have seen God's Spirit at work this week. How have you experienced grace in a new way through Christian practice? Discuss any joys or struggles you had. How is it with your soul?

 **urpose**

Because we long for Christ to be formed in us, we make this covenant to tend the fires of our souls so that our longing for Christ may never be extinguished and that our lives will be set ablaze with his love.

 **nstruction**

Most congregational worship contains a prayer of confession, even if they don't call it that. During this prayer time, the community as a whole confesses the sins of the world to God. We come before God on behalf of creation to plead forgiveness for our abuse of the earth, our neglect of the poor and hurting, our distrust of one another, and our lack of faith.

Why Confession?

❖ Name some reasons why prayers of confession are included in Christian worship.

❖ What is different about a group of people acknowledging sin instead of individuals privately talking to God about sin?

❖ Is it helpful to say a prayer of confession out loud in the midst of a Christian community? Why?

❖ Does it matter if every word of the corporate prayer fits your personal situation? Why?

Together write a prayer of confession for your small group of believers. Brainstorm what would be important to include. Make the prayer general instead of specific, not including names of certain people. Pray the prayer together. You also might submit it to your pastor for use in a Sunday worship service.

We're All in the Same Boat

Some of us may have too low an opinion of ourselves; others think too highly of ourselves. The reality is that every human being has moments of breaking our relationship with God or other persons. None of us is "better" or "worse"; we all need forgiveness.

Read the story of the woman caught in adultery (John 8:3-11).

❖ What do you think this story says to us about how we live together in community?

❖ Can you think of a time in your own life when you were tempted to judge another person? Have you ever felt judged by others?

You Got That?

Jesus spoke frequently about forgiveness. Even after he was crucified, died, and had spent three days in a tomb, Jesus came back to his disciples with the same important message. Read John 20:19-23.

❖ Why do you think Jesus said this to those who gathered in a locked room?

❖ What do you think is the importance of bowing before God as a community seeking forgiveness?

 ehearsal

Divide into two groups and read Jeremiah 3:1-18 as a litany. One group will read verses 1-5 and the other group reads verses 6-18. God calls Israel to confess, repent, and be restored. God calls us as the church today to do the same.

nvolving

What kind of ripples might (or have) come about from practicing confession and forgiveness? How could your daily routine change by the transformation taking place in your soul? Discuss how you might see all areas of your life—home, school, nature, community, world, job, paying bills, and so forth—connected in a new way based on your spiritual formation journey.

omorrow

❑ Read Colossians 3:12-17, then write in your journal about which areas still need your attention in your spiritual growth.

❑ Memorize this verse from Psalm 103:11: "For as the heavens are high above the earth, so great is his steadfast love toward those who fear him; as far as the east is from the west, so far he removes our transgressions from us."

❑ Write a prayer of confession and share it with your pastor this week; see if he or she would be willing to let you lead the prayer in worship.

❑ In worship, pay special attention as the prayer of confession is read. Did you have a new experience praying it this week? Journal about the worship.

> "'I will not be angry forever. Only acknowledge your guilt—you have rebelled against the LORD your God, and you have scattered your favors to foreign gods under every spreading tree, and have not obeyed me,'" declares the LORD.
> —Jeremiah 3:12b-13 (NIV)

Healing Prayers and Hands

 **igns of the Spirit**

Discuss where you have seen God's Spirit at work this week. How have you experienced grace in a new way through Christian practice? Discuss any joys or struggles you had. How is it with your soul?

 **urpose**

Because we long for Christ to be formed in us, we make this covenant to tend the fires of our souls so that our longing for Christ may never be extinguished and that our lives will be set ablaze with his love.

> And these signs will accompany those who believe ... they will lay their hands on the sick, and they will recover.
> —Mark 16:17a, 18

 **nstruction**

Have you ever witnessed a miraculous healing? ever said a prayer for the health and well-being of a sick friend? ever kissed a toddler's sore finger or kept a bedside vigil with loved ones? Have you ever experienced the power of healing prayers and hands in your life? Discuss any healing experiences you have had.

As believers, we ask God for healing mercies. We gather to pray, to anoint, and to lay hands on those in pain. Our prayers reassure and point to the presence of God with us. Our touch reminds the patient of the healing touch of Jesus.

God couples the prayers and compassionate gestures of believers with other gifted hands, heads, and hearts to bring about health and well-being. It is God who kisses and makes it better.

The Prayers We Pray

Talk together about how you have experienced prayers for healing.

❖ When do you hear prayers for the sick and those who mourn?
❖ Are you invited to pray for the healing of others during worship?
❖ How do you sense God's presence and power in intercessory prayers for healing?

❖ What feelings do you have as people ask for prayers for the healing of specific persons?

❖ Have you ever asked for healing prayers for yourself or for someone you love?

Do You Believe?

The disciples' efforts to heal a boy had failed (Mark 9:14-29). Doubt and skepticism seemed reasonable. The father was desperate. Jesus questioned the father's belief. Picture the father's hands folded with his fingers intertwined. He answers as if one hand believes while the other hand doubts. Read aloud the passage from Mark 9.

> Jesus said to him, "If you are able!—All things can be done for the one who believes." Immediately the father of the child cried out, "I believe; help my unbelief!"
> —Mark 9:23-24

❖ Have you ever cried out like this father? What was the situation?

❖ What is the connection between healing prayers and hands and a strong community of faith?

Prayers and Presence

The presence of believers with the sick and distressed makes room for the light of Christ. This light reveals the pain, gives ear to the sighs, and steps in to make all things possible.

Healing prayers, anointing, and laying on of hands are acts of compassion and mercy. The spiritual practice of healing is a ministry of presence. We listen carefully to those in pain. We pray for God's healing and wholeness. We touch and bear the healing light of Christ.

Spend a few quiet moments listening to the confident assurance of God's voice. Write a response to this affirmation of God's faithfulness and love.

Read aloud the story of Jesus' healing a paralytic from Luke 5:17-26. What does this story tell us about God's healing hands? How might we gain access to that heavenly power? Discuss with a partner and write your thoughts below.

Soul-Tending: Life-Forming Practices for Older Youth & Young Adults

Does God Say No?

Sometimes because we pray for healing, we expect that God will heal our loved ones, either physically or spiritually. Then when what we expected doesn't happen, we blame God for not answering our prayers.

❖ Do you think God answers prayer even when things go differently than you hoped?

❖ How is God's plan sometimes different than what we think it should be?

❖ How can God's healing occur, even if a physical body is not healed?

> Give ear to my words, O LORD; give heed to my sighing. Listen to the sound of my cry, my King and my God, for to you I pray.
> —Psalm 5:1-2

 ehearsal

In communities of faith, God uses the hearts and hands of the church to reach out with healing. Make a list of persons in your community who need physical or spiritual healing. Take time now to pray for them by name.

Pray a liturgy of healing together. Choose a brief service of healing from your denomination's book of worship or from resources recommended by your pastor. Together, pray the liturgy.

 nvolving

What kind of ripples might (or have) come about from praying for healing? How could your daily routine change by the transformation taking place in your soul? Discuss how you might see all areas of your life—home, school, nature, community, world, job, paying bills, and so forth—connected in a new way based on your spiritual formation journey.

# Tomorrow

- ❏ Intercessory prayer—praying into the lives of others—is healing prayer. Many communities of faith have a prayer chain that operates around the clock. Phone calls and emails connect those who pray for the health and well-being of others. Volunteer on a prayer chain or get online and create your own.

- ❏ Practice the spiritual discipline of healing in community. Gather believers for a time of healing prayers, anointing, and the laying on of hands.

- ❏ Put your healing hands to work in practical and compassionate ways. Check with your area hospital or hospice house. Many are in need of volunteers who would offer time and a healing touch. You might rock a baby, rub feet, or stroke a hand. Pray as you do and invite others to pray their way into the lives of those you touch.

- ❏ Start a prayer journal. Keep track of persons as you pray into their lives. Pay attention to what God does with the prayers of believers and with the gifted hands, heads, and hearts of doctors and other trained health specialists. Witness to the healing light of Christ. Give thanks and praise in the company of other believers.

- ❏ Be trained as a Stephen Minister. Check *www.stephenministries.org* or call 314-428-2600 for more information.

- ❏ Call The Upper Room Prayer Center to see how you can be involved in this healing ministry. Find them at their website, *www.upperroom.org*.

> Are any among you sick? They should call for the elders of the church and have them pray over them, anointing them with oil in the name of the Lord. The prayer of faith will save the sick, and the Lord will raise them up; and anyone who has committed sins will be forgiven.
>
> —James 5:14-15

Soul-Tending: Life-Forming Practices for Older Youth & Young Adults

Loving Hospitality

Signs of the Spirit

Discuss where you have seen God's Spirit at work this week. How have you experienced grace in a new way through Christian practice? Discuss any joys or struggles you had. How is it with your soul?

Purpose

Because we long for Christ to be formed in us, we make this covenant to tend the fires of our souls so that our longing for Christ may never be extinguished and that our lives will be set ablaze with his love.

Be hospitable to one another without complaining.
—I Peter 4:9

Instruction

What's the first thing that pops into your head when you think of hospitality? Do you think of beautiful parties? frantic preparations? five-star restaurants? the pleasant warmth of a hotel jacuzzi?

The spiritual practice of loving hospitality is about accepting the desperate phone calls in the middle of the night. It's about welcoming the lost and making room for travelers. It's about belonging and having a place at the table. Hospitality is the warmth of love given and received.

Host and Guest

The Greek word *xenos* means both host and guest. The root word of hospitality—*hospes*—claims both the host and guest as one. Martha received Jesus as a guest (Luke 10:38). After he had received Martha's gift of hospitality, he became the host and offered his own gifts to Mary. The men along the road to Emmaus (Luke 24:13-35) offered to host and feed a "stranger." Jesus turned the tables on their hospitality and became the host by breaking the bread.

Is Jesus just a bad guest? What do you think of this table-turning hospitality? Talk about your experience as both host and guest. As a host, what do you give? How does your hospitality make room for your guests to give? When have you turned the table on a guest? Have you, as a guest, ever found yourself in the host's chair?

Making Room

From beginning to end, the Scriptures call us to love our neighbor. Words of the law direct God's chosen ones to love the stranger, open our hearts and hands to the poor and needy, and eat with our enemies. The gospel summons believers to welcome and give care to the least. The call is not in question. How to carry out the call is in question. Discuss the following:

❖ How do you swing the door open wide enough to embrace your neighbor?

❖ How does your worshipping community make room to love and care for all human beings?

Sometimes the door slams on hospitality. After the events of Christ's crucifixion and resurrection, fear forced the disciples to lock the door. Fear kept the disciples a "safe distance" away from danger. Their fear also kept them in "safe closeness" apart from all that threatened them. Take a minute or two and discuss the fears that make you slam the door in the face of others in need. What other feelings keep you from answering knocks? Write down any thoughts or insights you have.

> When it was evening on that day, the first day of the week, and the doors of the house where the disciples had met were locked for fear of the Jews, Jesus came and stood among them and said, "Peace be with you."
> —John 20:19

Jesus calls us to overcome our fears and be hospitable to all persons. We are to reach out to help those in need, and do the simple things like be a listening ear when needed. God's love smothers us with a genuine concern for all persons when we have the doors of our hearts open to receiving that love. When our hearts are open, our doors are too.

Jesus stood among the disciples. He offered peace in exchange for their fears and anxious feelings. This peace has the power to change *hostis* (enemy) into *hospes* (guest). Is God knocking on another door? Make room to open it!

 ehearsal

Evaluate your group's capacity for offering loving hospitality.

❖ Develop a strategy for welcoming persons to your group.

- ❖ When guests come, you can help them eventually sit in the host's chair. Guests just need a chance to offer their gifts: to tell stories, to display their art, or to share something new.
- ❖ Jot notes of welcome to friends and family who are not a part of a small group or worshipping community.

nvolving

What kind of ripples might (or have) come about from practicing loving hospitality? How could your daily routine change by the transformation taking place in your soul? Discuss how you might see all areas of your life—home, school, nature, community, world, job, paying bills, and so forth—connected in a new way based on your spiritual formation journey.

omorrow

> You shall also love the stranger, for you were strangers in the land of Egypt.
> —Deuteronomy 10:19

❑ Strangers become friends at the Lord's table. The familiar actions and stories make room for us to accept and receive. We welcome one another and Christ into our lives as the bread and cup are lifted and shared. Seek an opportunity to share the sacrament of Holy Communion as a guest at another church.

❑ At one time or another, we are all strangers. Pray the Scripture from Deuteronomy. Invite God to give you a stranger's insight into loving hospitality. Listen for ways you might reach out to someone—as one stranger to another.

❑ Form a hospitality team in your youth group, campus fellowship, or church. Volunteer to take food to shut-ins, to welcome visitors in the church, or do other acts of hospitality you can think of.

Acts of Justice and Reconciliation

 igns of the Spirit

Discuss where you have seen God's Spirit at work this week. How have you experienced grace in a new way through Christian practice? Discuss any joys or struggles you had. How is it with your soul?

 urpose

Because we long for Christ to be formed in us, we make this covenant to tend the fires of our souls so that our longing for Christ may never be extinguished and that our lives will be set ablaze with his love.

 nstruction

Society's Understanding of Justice

The family of a murder victim demands justice. The man accused of the crime demands justice from the court system, protecting his rights and guaranteeing him a fair trial. Pro-death penalty groups demand "sure and swift" justice for the accused.

Anti-death penalty groups assert that the man accused of the crime cannot receive justice because he is poor, and that the death penalty is an unjust punishment. The jury hearing the case is told that it is their responsibility to see that justice is served by fairly and impartially applying the law to the facts presented. Later appeals allege justice was denied in the case because the prosecutor acted unfairly, the defense counsel was incompetent, and the judge was biased. These are just a few of the ways the term justice is used everyday.

As a group, discuss the meanings of *justice* as the term is used above. List the meanings below:

The everyday understandings of justice are little help in understanding what constitutes "acts of justice" by the church. In order to determine what "acts of justice" are, we must examine the meaning of *justice* in Scripture.

Justice for the Powerless

Scripture first mentions *justice* in connection with God's purposes for Abraham, including being a blessing for all nations. "I have chosen ... [Abraham], that he may charge his children and his household after him to keep the way of the LORD by doing righteousness and justice" (Genesis 18:19a). The justice to be practiced by Abraham will be an example for the world.

Under the laws of Leviticus and Deuteronomy, justice is equated with giving honest testimony in legal proceedings, not showing partiality to either the poor or the rich (Leviticus 19:15; Deuteronomy 16:19). Also appearing for the first time in Deuteronomy is a theme that will define the concept of justice for later generations of Jews and Christians. Those in power have a duty to dispense justice, defined as fair treatment, compassion, and mercy for the weak and those with no power base. Thus, Deuteronomy admonishes the people to protect the rights of aliens, widows, and orphans (Deuteronomy 24:17; 27:19). Scripture reminds us that, when we forget these priorities, God hears and answers the cries of those we oppress (see Exodus 2:23-25; 22:27; and Psalm 34:17).

The prophets also equated justice with fair treatment of the powerless. Amos condemns those who trample the needy into the dirt and calls instead that they should "let justice roll down like waters, and righteousness like an ever-flowing stream" (Amos 5:24). Micah condemns the rulers who have perverted justice and equity (Micah 3:9-12). Micah then sums up the desire of God in three instructions. Read aloud the passage from Micah 6:8 and discuss this question:

❖ What is your understanding of justice in the Old Testament?

Christ came to establish God's justice. Scriptures considered by Christians to foretell the coming of Christ speak of the establishment of God's justice. "Here is my servant, whom I uphold, my chosen, in whom my soul delights; I have put my spirit upon him; he will bring forth justice to the nations" (Isaiah 42:1). The coming servant's justice will be a light to all the peoples (Isaiah 51:4). "In those days and at that time I will cause a righteous Branch to spring up for David; and he shall execute justice and righteousness in the land" (Jeremiah 33:15; see also Matthew 12:18).

Christians understand justice to mean that those members of society who are poor, sick, injured, incompetent, defenseless, and living on the margins will not be victimized and will be treated fairly and compassionately. Christians understand that God cares about justice, and that God hears the cries of the oppressed. When we deny justice, we deny God.

> He has told you, O mortal, what is good; and what does the LORD require of you but to do justice, and to love kindness, and to walk humbly with your God?
>
> —Micah 6:8

Work one or more of the following exercises:

❖ Identify those in your community who are powerless or particularly susceptible, for whatever reason, to being oppressed. Be as specific as possible, even identifying neighborhoods where such persons might live or might be found. Are you a member of any of these groups? Do you participate in the oppression of any of these persons?

❖ Discuss the use of the death penalty. Nothing is more human and fallible than the criminal justice system. No matter how much care is exercised by police, prosecutors, attorneys, judges, and juries, mistakes happen and some innocent people are convicted while some guilty people remain unpunished. Recognizing that there is biblical support both for and against capital punishment, how are Christians to speak to this issue of justice?

❖ Are the benefits you enjoy as a citizen or resident of the United States derived exclusively from your hard work or the hard work of those close to you? Do you believe that you, or those close to you, work harder and are more deserving than a peasant farmer in Africa or a child laborer in India? Does that belief make one an oppressor? Is that attitude an issue of justice? How?

❖ In 1999, a United Nations agency estimated that the richest twenty percent of the world is consuming more than eighty percent of the world's resources. Put another way, there are not enough resources to provide everyone with the standard of living many of us have come to take for granted. Based on your understanding of God's justice, do you believe that disparity is of concern to God? Why?

Discuss how your community of faith might find ways to be active in working for justice. How will your faith be strengthened and your soul be nurtured by working for justice and reconciliation?

 ehearsal

Assign parts based on the questions below, then role play the situations:

❖ Your church has organized a prayer vigil against the death penalty for the convicted murderer of a young woman you knew. The woman's family has asked you why your church wants to save the life of this murderer. What do you say to the family? Would you attend the vigil, knowing that your attendance might cause pain to the family?

❖ You enjoy playing the state-sponsored lottery. You only spend a few dollars a month, and it's exciting to listen as the winning numbers are announced. Then you learn that the state spends most of its advertising dollars targeted at the poorest members of the population, increasing the amount of advertising when government checks are typically mailed. You discover that many families are being hurt when family members develop

Soul-Tending: Life-Forming Practices for Older Youth & Young Adults

gambling addictions, squandering the family's money. You suggest to your Sunday school class that the church should get involved in putting an end to the lottery. No one else agrees with you. How do you explain to your fellow Christians that there are issues of justice involved?

nvolving

What kind of ripples might (or have) come about from practicing acts of justice and reconciliation? How could your daily routine change by the transformation taking place in your soul? Discuss how you might see all areas of your life—home, school, nature, community, world, job, paying bills, and so forth—connected in a new way based on your spiritual formation journey.

omorrow

❑ Watch several different news programs daily, praying for God's justice. Identify current events that involve issues of justice and any groups that appear to be victimized, including:
  ❖ issues of taxation
  ❖ criminal legislation
  ❖ embargoes against other nations
  ❖ news and legislation regarding aliens, the homeless, or the mentally incompetent

❑ Find out how you could join your church's local, regional, or national ministry engaging in justice concerns.

❑ Read the Book of Amos. List those acts that Amos might condemn if he walked through our cities today. Pray about these issues. What is God calling you to do about these situations?

❑ If your state uses capital punishment, contact your local bar associations to find out what funds are available to pay for attorneys and investigators for the defense of capital cases and for their prosecution. Pray that the attorneys would seek God's justice in each case.

❑ Pray daily that God will show you injustice in the world and help you discern what the church can do to address these concerns.

Ordination

 **igns of the Spirit**

Discuss where you have seen God's Spirit at work this week. How have you experienced grace in a new way through Christian practice? Discuss any joys or struggles you had. How is it with your soul?

 **urpose**

Because we long for Christ to be formed in us, we make this covenant to tend the fires of our souls so that our longing for Christ may never be extinguished and that our lives will be set ablaze with his love.

> Then I heard the voice of the Lord saying, "Whom shall I send, and who will go for us?"
> And I said, "Here am I; send me!"
> —Isaiah 6:8

 **nstruction**

Have you ever felt called to ministry? Perhaps someone has asked you that question. Maybe you've wondered about it yourself. The idea may seem strange or frightening or unappealing: *Me—ordained to be a minister?*

All Are Called

Christians believe that all disciples of Jesus are called to some form of ministry. When we are baptized and when we claim our baptism through confirmation or a profession of faith, responding to this calling is a part of our response. We are given different spiritual gifts (1 Corinthians 12) in order to build up the body of Christ (Ephesians 4). Some minister as schoolteachers, as nurses and physicians, as businessmen and businesswomen, and as computer technicians and mechanics.

❖ Can you think of someone in your community whose work in the world is a ministry?

❖ What is the ministry to which you are called right now?

We also believe that God calls some to ordained ministry. The call may not be in an audible voice. I had pursued several other paths in college, and none seemed to lead me anywhere. One summer, while working on a camp staff, I had the sense that I should serve full-time in Christian ministry. And when I said yes to this leading, I felt an inner peace.

❖ Have you or do you know of someone who had a clear sense of a "call" to ordained ministry?

Some Are Set Apart

Ordained ministry begins with the call of God, sometimes identified as an "inner call." This inner call is usually "echoed" in an outer call. Faithful friends, family, teachers, and leaders are good people to talk with about a call of God in our lives. The church can also affirm our call. In this way the call of God may become audible, as God speaks to the individual through the church. When a person is ordained, he or she is "set apart" for specific service to God. God calls certain people to lead others in their faith walks.

❖ Why would it be important for someone to have others confirm his or her inner call to ministry?

Young women and men exploring ordination are given mentors who help them discern and pray about this direction for their lives. They are not in this journey alone. The call to ordained ministry is also a call to prepare. College and seminary courses in religion and theology build a solid foundation, and internships give candidates practical experience.

The Power Belongs to God

Candidates for ordination also develop relationships with ordained men and women. They find them to be human, with faults, failures, and sins but also with commitments to seek God's will in the work they are about.

One of the heresies of the early church was that the priest had to be perfect for the Communion service to be valid. Instead, the Bible reminds us that we have the treasure of the gospel of Jesus Christ in "clay jars, so that it may be made clear that this extraordinary power belongs to God and does not come from us" (2 Corinthians 4:7).

God uses ordinary men and women in the work of ordained ministry. Some are effective speakers, while others are not. Some are great listeners, while others are not. Some are evangelists, missionaries, teachers, and organizers—all of these gifts can be of service to God and the world.

All Christians are called to some form of ministry. What is God saying to you? How will you respond?

 ehearsal

Take some time to discuss what it might be like to be an ordained minister.

❖ List some reasons a person might give for not being an ordained minister. List some other reasons for serving as an ordained minister. Compare your lists with others.

❖ Describe the ideal ordained minister. What would she or he be like?

❖ What is the most important part of an ordained minister's job?

❖ Which persons of your own age group have talents or characteristics that would make them good ordained ministers?

Then discuss how God might be calling you to ministry, even if it is not ordination. Where will you go for God? Sing together the hymn, "Here I Am, Lord" or another song about answering God's call.

nvolving

What kind of ripples might (or have) come about from practicing ordination? How could your daily routine change by the transformation taking place in your soul? Discuss how you might see all areas of your life—home, school, nature, community, world, job, paying bills, and so forth—connected in a new way based on your spiritual formation journey.

omorrow

❑ Schedule a conversation with an ordained minister about his or her work. What is satisfying about the job? What is sustaining? What is most important to him or her about the work of a minister?

❑ Have a conversation with an adult whose judgment and wisdom have helped you in the past. Ask him or her to pray with you and to listen as you talk about different paths of ministry that might be in your future.

❑ Ask to "shadow" (follow alongside) an ordained minister as he or she works one afternoon. Discuss the experience afterward.

❑ Memorize Isaiah 6:8, meditating upon the ministry to which God is sending you.

Spiritual Friendship

igns of the Spirit

Discuss where you have seen God's Spirit at work this week. How have you experienced grace in a new way through Christian practice? Discuss any joys or struggles you had. How is it with your soul?

urpose

Because we long for Christ to be formed in us, we make this covenant to tend the fires of our souls so that our longing for Christ may never be extinguished and that our lives will be set ablaze with his love.

nstruction

Most of us have friends with whom we enjoy hanging out, but what takes a friendship to a deeper level? Perhaps two people undergo a difficult situation or trauma together, or on the other side, share such great joy that they are bound to each other. Maybe the friends are compatible and develop a level of trust that enables each to share the deep recesses of their hearts. Other friends may have known each other so long they can finish each other's sentences. Friends are an important and beautiful part of life. Take a minute to discuss great friendships of which you have been a part.

> ❖ What makes a good friendship?

> ❖ What do you think of when you hear the words *spiritual friendship*?

Friends in the Spirit

In the Christian church, there is a long tradition of spiritual friendship as a way to grow closer to God. What is a "spiritual friend"? How is a spiritual friendship different from other close friendships? In any close friendship, two people will share what is most important in their lives: hopes, dreams, fears, and concerns about relationships, as well as details of their everyday lives. In a spiritual friendship two people may also share such things, but in addition there will be a stated focus on each person's relationship with God.

John Wesley used to ask, "How is it with your soul?" That is a good starting point for a spiritual friendship. In spiritual friendship people agree to share about their spiritual lives in a way that encourages each one's growth in God. They might set aside a regular time to talk about what is happening in their prayer lives, how the words of a sermon struck them, or an image that came during a period of silence.

Beginning a Spiritual Friendship

Spiritual friends trust each other and pledge to keep conversations confidential. They practice holy listening and simple joys together. Your goal will be to each know God better and grow on your individual spiritual journeys. Discuss the following questions and write down any insights you have:

> The soul of Jonathan was bound to the soul of David, and Jonathan loved him as his own soul.
> —1 Samuel 18:1b

❖ Do you think spiritual friendships between young persons can work? Why or why not?

❖ Why is it important to have a special person to whom you can talk about your relationship with God?

❖ Turn to a partner and discuss the following:
I am closest to God when _____.
I would describe my spiritual life as _____.
My faith is tested by _____.
I sometimes wonder if God is calling me to _____.

Read Luke 1:39-45, then discuss:

❖ What was Mary's relationship to Elizabeth?

❖ Why do you think Mary wanted to go for a visit at that particular time?

❖ Based on this Scripture passage, why do you think spiritual friendship is so important to the life of our faith?

❖ Which close friends recognize blessings in your life and point them out to you?

rehearsal

Listening With Your Spirit

Spiritual friends may not call it this, but they hear what the other is saying by holy listening. In this way the one who is speaking is heard, understood, and prayed for by the listener. How many friends really listen to you when you talk? How well do you listen when your friends talk? To be a spiritual friend, you must listen well—and you have the freedom to do that because you know that you'll have a chance to be fully heard.

Practice this exercise with a spiritual friend:

Divide into pairs. This process may seem rather scripted, but by practicing your listening skills you will learn to be a spiritual friend. Begin with a minute of silence.

Speaker one has five minutes to talk about "Where do I see God in my life right now?" The listener remains prayerfully silent for these five minutes.

Another minute of silence will give both persons a chance to reflect on how they are feeling.

The second speaker has five minutes to talk about "Where do I see God in my life right now?" The listener remains prayerfully silent for these five minutes.

Take one more minute of silence.

Discuss your answers to these questions with your partner:

❖ How did I feel as a listener? As a speaker?
❖ How was God present in our conversation?
❖ Write about your experience below.

 nvolving

What kind of ripples might (or have) come about from practicing spiritual friendship? How could your daily routine change by the transformation taking place in your soul? Discuss how you might see all areas of your life—home, school, nature, community, world, job, paying bills, and so forth—connected in a new way based on your spiritual formation journey.

 omorrow

❏ Think of who might be a possible spiritual friend for you. If no one immediately comes to mind, ask God to help you find a person who can help you grow spiritually.

❏ Take time to journal about what you might want and need in a spiritual friendship. List any of the questions you have in your faith journey or issues you face in your relationship with God.

❏ Read about David and Jonathan (1 Samuel 18:1-4; 23:15-18). How was theirs a spiritual friendship? Have you had any friendship that similarly encouraged you to know God better? Thank God for your spiritual friend in prayer each day this week.

❏ Write down what qualities you think are most important in a spiritual friend. Then make an honest appraisal of yourself: In what ways could you be a good spiritual friend to someone else? Are there aspects of yourself that might need to change before you could open yourself to another's intimate journey with God?

❏ Read and meditate on the story of Mary and Elizabeth each day this week. How is their spiritual friendship an example and a blessing for you?

Soul-Tending: Life-Forming Practices for Older Youth & Young Adults

Being the Body of Christ

igns of the Spirit

Discuss where you have seen God's Spirit at work this week. How have you experienced grace in a new way through Christian practice? Discuss any joys or struggles you had. How is it with your soul?

urpose

Because we long for Christ to be formed in us, we make this covenant to tend the fires of our souls so that our longing for Christ may never be extinguished and that our lives will be set ablaze with his love.

nstruction

Leader to the people: "He has risen."
People: "He has risen indeed."
Second in importance only to the words, *he is risen,* are these words: *Now you are the body of Christ and individually members of it* (1 Corinthians 12:27). In this age when many Christians emphasize personal salvation or a personal relationship with Jesus Christ, it is important to remember these words of Paul. We are the body of Christ.

Describe a human body. Note its properties. List its attributes, its needs, and how it functions. List its strengths and weaknesses. What improves its performance and functionality? What harms the body? Now make another list, substituting the word *church* for the term *human body*. Discuss the parallels.

About as Human as You Can Get

A source of great frustration yet great comfort is the reality that the church is about as human as you can get. All the sins of humanity are played out in the church. This fact is a source of frustration because Christians, quite understandably and properly, expect the church, the body of Christ, to rise above our sinful natures. It is also a source of comfort because despite our shortfalls and weaknesses, God has made us the body of Christ and enables us to be the presence of Christ in the world.

❖ Discuss with a partner: How is the church to be the presence of Christ in the world if it is subject to human sins and failings?

Paul tells us to clothe ourselves in love, letting the peace of Christ rule in our hearts, treat one another as brothers and sisters, and make everything we do something we do in the name of Jesus Christ (Colossians 3:14-17).

The Greatest of These Is Love

Paul tells the church, "Love!" "Let love be genuine; hate what is evil, hold fast to what is good; love one another with mutual affection" (Romans 12:9-10). "Owe no one anything, except to love one another" (Romans 13:8). "Knowledge puffs up, but love builds up" (1 Corinthians 8:1b). "Live in love, as Christ loved us" (Ephesians 5:2). There are many more Scripture passages that speak of loving others. The point is this: You do not devote that much ink to something that is not important. The guiding principle of conduct for the body of Christ is love.

First Corinthians 13, the so-called "love chapter," is often read at weddings. However, Paul was not writing to a newly married couple but to the church at Corinth and to us, the body of Christ. Read the Scripture passage aloud. In pairs apply the teachings of this chapter to congregations you have experienced. Discuss the ways these faith communities have acted with love and ways they have failed to act with love.

Brothers and Sisters

At one time it was common for people in the church to address one another as "brother" and "sister." The practice still exists in some traditions and has biblical roots. Paul used the words over one hundred twenty times to address his churches, the body of Christ. In contrast, he only used the term *saints* about forty times.

If we speak and come to think of one another as brothers and sisters—as family—we are more likely to act toward one another with love and care. Paul's use of "brother" and "sister" was quite intentional. Paul wished the church, the body of Christ, to understand itself as a family with Christ as its head.

Do It in the Name of Christ

A slogan heard in churches today is "WWJD: What would Jesus do?" While this question has potential to motivate good behavior, a more challenging and meaningful standard to measure conduct is offered by Paul: "Whatever you do, in word or deed, do everything in the name of the Lord Jesus, giving thanks to God the Father through him" (Colossians 3:17).

Take a moment and think of some of the unloving, hateful things you have done. Perhaps the unkind words spoken in anger, the gossip you couldn't resist spreading, or the thoughtless neglect of some simple act of kindness come to mind. Now imagine saying, before you committed these acts, "I am doing this in the name of my Lord, Jesus Christ." Would you have committed those acts with those words on your lips? How would you feel about the acts if you had?

Soul-Tending: Life-Forming Practices for Older Youth & Young Adults

Understanding yourself as part of the body of Christ means that those words are implied in everything you say and do. When you act out of love, you do so in the name of Christ. When you act out of hate, you do so in the name of Christ. You can't blame the bad acts on an evil twin. The good you do builds and strengthens the body of Christ. The evil you do tears down and weakens the body of Christ. Discuss your thoughts about the body of Christ and write them below.

Bringing It All Together

The body of Christ is a creation of and powered by the Spirit of God. When it operates at its best, it is a family—brothers and sisters—led by Christ, acting in the name of Christ, out of love for each other and love for God's creation.

Years ago, a cartoonist named Rube Goldberg drew cartoons of strange and complex gadgets, machines that filled whole rooms. Windmills or mice on treadmills might operate these strange contraptions. They contained countless wheels and pulleys, gears turning clockwise and counterclockwise. They were always designed to perform a simple task: a room-sized machine that buttered a piece of toast and a room-sized machine that turned on a light "automatically," for example. "Rube Goldberg Device" came to mean a complicated, inefficient, and impractical device or organization.

The church is often God's "Rube Goldberg Device." Conflicted, inefficient, totally broken down in parts, it operates only because God wills it to. The miracle of Christ's presence is confirmed in the reality that God has preserved the church, in all its brokenness, for more than two thousand years; and the church, in all its brokenness, ministers to the world.

Yet in the church is an unrealized potential that is achievable through the power of God. When parts of the church come to understand themselves as the body of Christ, the living presence of Christ, acting out of love and in the name of Jesus Christ, the world sees the presence of Christ. The gospel is proclaimed in a manner that is apparent to all. The dream, the goal, is the realization of that potential throughout the entire body of Christ.

 ehearsal

The church, as the body of Christ, is called to love God and neighbor. Dorotheos, a sixth century Christian monk, sought to demonstrate that loving God and neighbor was one command: If you love your neighbor, you love God; if you love God, you love your neighbor. His model for this principle has come to be known as Dorotheos' Compass (see page 188 for more information).

Stand in a circle at arms'
length, holding hands.
Imagine that God is present
in the center of the circle.
Have everyone take two steps
toward the center of the circle.

❖ What happens to the
space between the
members of the
group?

❖ What would happen
if you simply moved
closer to one another
in the circle?

❖ As a group, discuss
what it means to
place God at the
center of your life.

❖ How do we move
closer to God in our
lives? How do we
move closer to one
another in our lives?
How can the church
be the presence of
Christ to the world?

Suppose we were to take a compass and insert the
point and draw the outline of a circle. The center
point is the same distance from any point on the
circumference. Now concentrate your minds on what
is to be said! Let us suppose that this circle is the
world and that God himself is the center; the straight
lines drawn from the circumference are the lives of
men. To the degree that the saints enter into the
things of the spirit, they desire to come near to God;
and in proportion to their progress in the things of
the spirit they do in fact come closer to God and to
their neighbor. The closer they are to God, the closer
they are to one another; and the closer they are to
one another, the closer they become to God. Now
consider in the same context the question of
separation; for when they stand away from God and
turn to external things, it is clear that the more that
they recede and become distant from God, the more
they become distant from one another. See! This is
the very nature of love. The more we are turned away
from and do not love God, the greater the distance
that separates us from our neighbor. ... the more we
are united to our neighbor the more
we are united to God.

—Saint Dorotheos of Gaza, (Sixth Century),
from "To Love as God Loves"

 nvolving

What kind of ripples might (or have) come about from practicing being the body of Christ in the world? How could your daily routine change by the transformation taking place in your soul? Discuss how you might see all areas of your life—home, school, nature, community, world, job, paying bills, and so forth—connected in a new way based on your spiritual formation journey.

 omorrow

❑ Keep a journal listing everything you have done over the day. Include conversations you had, disagreements with others, acts of ministry, or anything that occurred. Understanding that we do everything in the name of Christ, use a colored marker to highlight those things that you believe God could use to strengthen the body of Christ. Using a different color, highlight those that you believed weakened the body of Christ. Pray about both.

❑ For the next week, watch or listen to several different news programs each day. Read a newspaper daily. Take notes on current events that demonstrate the body of Christ in action. Also look for stories that you believe reflect poorly on the body of Christ. At the end of the week, review all your notes. How visible is the body of Christ in the news media and how is the body of Christ portrayed?

❑ A great irony is the fragmentation of the body of Christ into many different Christian traditions. Using a phone book, identify five different Christian traditions represented in your area. Go to the Internet and find websites sponsored by these traditions. Review their statements of beliefs. Pick one or two of these traditions and list four or five ways the beliefs of the tradition differ from your tradition and four or five ways they are the same. Try to determine if you could worship together, sharing the sacrament of the Lord's Supper.

❑ Pray daily for the body of Christ in all its unity and in all its brokenness.

Appendix

Recommended Resources

Contemporary Readings

The Art of Personal Prayer, by Lance Webb (Upper Room, 1977).

Celebration of Discipline: The Path to Spiritual Growth (Revised edition), by Richard J. Foster (HarperCollins Publishers, 1988).

Companions in Christ: A Small-Group Experience in Spiritual Formation, by Stephen D. Bryant, Janice T. Grana, and Marjorie J. Thompson (Upper Room, 2001).

Devotional Classics: Selected Readings For Individuals & Groups, edited by Richard J. Foster and James Bryan Smith (HarperCollins Publishers, San Francisco, 1990).

Devotional Life in the Wesleyan Tradition, by Steve Harper (Upper Room, 1999).

Disciplines of the Holy Spirit, by Siang-Yang Tan and Douglas H. Gregg (Zondervan Publishing House, 1997).

Eight Life-Enriching Practices of United Methodists, by Henry H. Knight III (Abingdon Press, 2001).

Embracing the Love of God: The Path and Promise of Christian Life, by James Bryan Smith and Richard J. Foster (Harper San Francisco, 1995).

Freedom of Simplicity, by Richard J. Foster (Harper & Row Publishers, San Francisco, 1981).

Hearing God: Developing a Conversational Relationship With God, by Dallas Willard (Intervarsity Press, 1999).

Invitation to Christian Spirituality: An Ecumenical Anthology, edited by John R. Tyson (Oxford Press, 1999).

Jesus Freaks, by dc Talk (Albury Publishers, 1999).

New Seeds of Contemplation, by Thomas Merton (New Directions, 1961).

Prayer: Finding the Heart's True Home, by Richard J. Foster (HarperCollins Publishers, 1992).

Songs for Renewal: A Devotion Guide to the Riches of Our Best-Loved Songs and Hymns, by Janet Lindeblad Janzen (Harper San Francisco, 1995).

Soul Feast: An Invitation to the Christian Spiritual Life, by Marjorie J. Thompson (Westminster John Knox, 1995).

The Spirit of the Disciplines: Understanding How God Changes Lives, by Dallas Willard (Harper San Francisco, 1991).

Spiritual Classics: Selected Readings for Individuals and Groups on the Twelve Spiritual Disciplines, edited by Richard J. Foster and Emilie Griffin (HarperCollins, 2000).

Study Guide for Celebration of Discipline, by Richard Foster (Harper & Row Publishers, 1983).

A Wesleyan Spiritual Reader, by Rueben P. Job (Abingdon Press, 1997).

When in Doubt, Sing: Prayer in Daily Life, by Jane Redmont (HarperCollins, 1999).

Yearning Minds and Burning Hearts: Rediscovering the Spirituality of Jesus, by Glandion Carney, William Long (Contributor) (Baker Books, 1997).

Classical Readings

The Cost of Discipleship, by Dietrich Bonhoeffer (Simon & Schuster Trade Paperbacks, 1976).

Experiencing the Depths of Jesus Christ, by Madame Jeanne Guyon (Thomas Nelson, 2000).

The Fruits of the Spirit, by Evelyn Underhill (Morehouse Publishing, 1982).

The Heart of Wesley's Journal, by John Wesley (McGraw-Hill Trade, 1979).

The Imitation of Christ, by Thomas à Kempis, translated by William C. Creasy (Catholic Book Publishing Company, 1997).

The Journal of John Woolman and a PLEA for the Poor, by John Woolman (Wipf & Stock Publishers, 1998).

Julian of Norwich: Showings, edited by Edmund Colledge, James Walsh, and Jean LeClercq (Paulist Press, 1988).

The Little Flowers of St. Francis, translated by Raphael Brown (Doubleday & Company, Incorporated, 1989).

Mere Christianity, by C. S. Lewis (Harper San Francisco, 2001).

Practicing His Presence, by Brother Lawrence and Frank C. Laubach (The Seedsowers, 1988).

The Soul's Delight: Selected Writings of Evelyn Underhill (Upper Room Spiritual Classics, 1998).

The Spiritual Formation Bible: New Revised Standard Version (Zondervan, 1999).

A Testament of Devotion, by Thomas Kelly (Harper San Francisco, 1996).

Books for Youth Workers

Caring From the Inside Out: How to Help Youth Show Compassion (SkillAbilities for Youth Ministry Series), by Soozung Sa (Abingdon Press, 1997).

The Christian Educator's Handbook of Spiritual Formation, edited by Kenneth O. Gangel and James C. Wilhoit (Baker Books, 1998).

Deepening Youth Spirituality: The Youth Worker's Guide, by Walt Marcum (Abingdon Press, 2001).

The Godbearing Life: The Art of Soul Tending for Youth Ministry, by Kenda Creasy Dean and Ron Foster (Upper Room Books, 1998).

Helping Youth Pray: How to Connect Youth With God (SkillAbilities for Youth Ministry Series), by Greg McKinnon (Abingdon Press, 1997).

Websites
(At the time of publication, all website addresses were correct and operational. Addresses may change in the future.)

www.ccel.org

ileadyouth.com

www.methodx.net

www.renovare.org

www.upperroom.org

www.taize.fr/en/index.htm

192